W9-CPZ-759

"Rosen applies a large dollop of humor, much of it self-directed, to his recounting of [his years coaching the Continental Basketball Association]. The shining star here isn't Rosen or any of the players, it's the game itself. The last half-dozen pages will bring a tear to the eye of anyone for whom the game was—or is—a passion."

—Wes Lukowsky, *Booklist* starred review

"Fast-paced, fanatical, and broken up by snippets of good-natured humor. . . . *Crazy Basketball* [is] a great read, for any casual basketball lover, insight into the former crazy league, but also a crazy coach who was a touch softened by it. For [Charley] Rosen, it was not only the Crazy Basketball Association, but his crazy association with basketball."

—Krystina Lucido, *Press Box*

"[Rosen's] journey from the [College Basketball Association] to a desk at Fox Sports is a one-of-a-kind basketball story—only to be believed in the words of the guy who actually lived it."

—*Foreword*

Praise for Charley Rosen's *Perfectly Awful: The Philadelphia 76ers' Horrendous and Hilarious 1972–1973 Season*

"The literature of sport usually focuses on championship teams and players. But the road to the top is littered with vanquished foes. The '72–'73 76ers are the ultimate vanquished foe. Great reading."

—Wes Lukowsky, *Booklist* starred review

"Charley Rosen's *Perfectly Awful* provides an insider's summary of the worst season in NBA history. His anecdotes and knowledge of the game give the reader an enlightening sense of the pre-merger NBA of the early 1970s, and of the 1972–73 Philadelphia 76ers, still the team most associated with losing by American sports fans."

—Bob Epling, *Aethlon: The Journal of Sports Literature*

THE CHOSEN GAME

The Chosen Game

A Jewish Basketball History

....

CHARLEY ROSEN

University of Nebraska Press · LINCOLN AND LONDON

CIP information can be found online at
https://lccn.loc.gov.2017017415.

Set in Lyon by Rachel Gould.
Designed by N. Putens.

The Jews were the first ethnic group to embrace basketball, and it's still a Jewish game.

—SONNY HILL, December 2, 2014

CONTENTS

PREFACE

Promise in the Promised Land

With his appearance wearing a Sacramento Kings uniform in the team's opening game of the 2006–7 season, Omri Casspi became the first Israeli-born hooper to play in the National Basketball Association (NBA). During his initial six years in what players call the League, Casspi proved to be a useful, if not a star-quality, performer. Still, as someone who's at least as interested in his Jewish heritage as he is in his on-court performance, Casspi famously connected his two passions in the summer of 2015.

That's when he arranged for three of his Sacramento teammates (DeMarcus Cousins, Rudy Gay, and Caron Butler), along with several other of his NBA contemporaries (Chandler Parsons, Tyreke Evans, Iman Shumpert, and Alan Anderson), to undertake a weeklong visit to Casspi's homeland. "You sit around a locker room, and you talk about your home," said Casspi. "I always tell my teammates, 'Come see my side of the world. I go to your houses. Come meet my parents, my brother, my sister.' It's literally as simple as that. On CNN, all you see is war. 'Come see for yourself.'"

Escorted everywhere by a security detail, the players' itinerary included visits to Jerusalem and the Holocaust Museum as well as a breakfast meeting with Prime Minister Benjamin Netanyahu. Followed by several dozen admiring youngsters wherever they went, the players also floated in the Dead Sea and, adhering to tradition, slipped personal messages into cracks in the Western Wall. Yet for Casspi, the most meaningful events were a pair of basketball clinics attended by a mixed group of Israeli and Palestinian youths.

Inevitably, however, the political implications of the trip could not be ignored. Although Casspi bore most of the financial burden, a chartered Boeing 747 was provided by casino mogul Sheldon Adelson, the multimillionaire supporter of Republican politicians and generous Israeli philanthropist. The trouble here was that among Adelson's virulent right-wing ideological ravings was his urging the United States to drop an atomic bomb on an uninhabited area of Iran as a show of force. Accordingly, several critics alleged that Casspi and Adelson organized the expedition in response to a Palestinian-founded campaign aimed at boycotting, isolating, and financially crippling Israel.

Casspi denied being motivated by the boycott campaign, saying, "Sheldon is a Republican, our president is a Democrat. Good, bad, whatever. It doesn't matter. . . . [This is] nothing about politics." What does matter, Casspi added, was to move young Israelis and young Palestinians toward peace and away from conflict. "That's why we're here. . . . I hope this helps."

While Casspi's venture was certainly unique, he merely followed the continuing tradition existing for well over a hundred years of pioneering Jewish players, coaches, and administrators who, either incidentally or deliberately, had a significant impact on the evolution of basketball as we know it, and therefore on the entire sports culture of America.

This, then, is the story of the chosen people and their chosen game.

THE CHOSEN GAME

1

....

In the Beginning

Dr. James Naismith was a thirty-one-year-old physical education teacher at the Young Men's Christian Association (YMCA) Training School in Springfield, Massachusetts, who, just before Christmas 1891,was charged with coming up with some kind of indoor activity to satisfy the raging hormones of his "rowdy" students.

His original thirteen rules of "Basket Ball" forbade running with the ball, as well as dribbling or kicking it. Since ball movement was limited to passing, the original Dr. J. believed that body contact would be minimized so that his students would be unlikely to injure one another. Naismith asked the janitor to find a pair of square baskets to be nailed to the track that overhung the gym, but only two circular peach baskets could be found. The track chanced to be ten feet above the gym floor, and the ball Naismith settled on was a soccer ball.

The inaugural contest was played on December 21, 1891, with nine players on each side. Fifteen minutes into the game, the first goal ever was made by William R. Chase, a sturdy young man wearing the requisite gray trousers and long-sleeved gray gym shirt and proudly displaying a small black mustache and a full head of slicked black hair. His historic shot was launched from twenty-five feet, certainly more of a baseball heave than a jump shot. The thirty-minute affair ended with a final score of 1-0.

During the subsequent Christmas holiday, the new game's enthusiastic participants introduced Basket Ball to their hometown friends. Within months several other YMCAs throughout the country also took up the game. Indeed, as many of Naismith's students began their career as Christian missionaries, Basket Ball was eventually introduced to China and various European countries.

Moreover, before the turn of the century, the joys of Naismith's invention began to be celebrated in Boston, Cleveland, and other urban areas. When the bouncing ball finally reached New York City, the game was adopted and eventually dominated by the numerous young Jewish men who lived there.

There were approximately 1,500 Jews living in America during the colonial era, mostly with Dutch Sephardic or English backgrounds. Another 100,000 Jews fled from Russia to the New World as a result of the six hundred anti-Semitic decrees issued by Czar Nicholas I during his thirty-year reign (1825–55). The next significant influx arrived from Germany in the aftermath of the failed 1848 socialist revolution. By 1881 this last group numbered around 250,000 and mostly consisted of professionals, journalists, and politicians.

Being highly educated, the German immigrants were easily assimilated into American culture to the point where in 1874, a Young Men's Hebrew Association (YMHA) was established on Manhattan's Lower East Side. This was an alternative to the several YMCAs in the city, which restricted Jewish membership to only 5 percent. In short order YMHAs were also chartered in Seattle, Chicago, Detroit, and Philadelphia.

In addition to offering literary, social, educational, and religious classes, these newly formed organizations also encouraged their members to participate in sports, because "athletics and Morality go hand in hand." More specifically, sports were a more desirable alternative to dance halls, nickelodeons, amusement parks, and other "disreputable entertainment" readily available in urban areas. This was something of a radically new concept, since European Jews rarely if ever participated in any kind of athletic endeavor. But any activity that would keep immigrant youths out of trouble was worth promoting.

As pogroms (Yiddish for "devastation" or "violent attacks") increased in frequency and brutality spread throughout Russia and Eastern Europe in the late nineteenth century, another wave of Jewish immigrants sought refuge in the land they called Golden Medinah (Golden Door). This latest influx mostly comprised illiterate peasants and uneducated laborers. The poverty, filth, and overall strangeness of these groups were seen by the already Americanized German immigrants as a threat to their own precarious security. To encourage and hasten the assimilation of these newcomers, the well-established German Americans founded several more YMHAs and community centers wherever these newcomers landed.

All told, the great majority of Jewish immigrants arrived and remained in New York City. By 1920 nearly half of all the Jews living in the United States resided in New York. As much as the young Jewish men and boys living on the Lower East Side sought some outlet for their athletic interests, the limited availability of public playing fields effectively ruled out baseball, football, and soccer. Also, the clubs and teams that played these outdoor sports on their own private turf accepted only Gentile members. On the other hand, there were several Jewish organizations that either owned or had access to small gymnasiums. By the process of elimination, then, Basket Ball became the athletic endeavor most favored by the thousands of young Jews living in New York City. Besides, the game was frenetic and required quick thinking, rapidity of movement, and endurance—making it the perfect urban sport.

Inevitably, several YMHAs in New York began to field basketball teams that, at first, competed against each other. Indeed, during the winter of 1896–97, the Brooklyn YMHA, powered by the play of Max Hess and F. P. Weil, soundly defeated all of its counterparts. With a new and deliberate intention of gaining respect from Gentiles, the Brooklyn YMHA team also played and bested several other squads that informally represented other ethnic organizations.

Fielding a successful basketball team became increasingly important for YMHAs, as the influx of Jewish immigrants created a backlash of virulent anti-Semitism in which the stereotypical Jew was seen as overly intellectual, crafty, small, and weak. Physically, they were depicted as being black haired, black eyed, thick lipped, swarthy complexioned, hook nosed, narrow chested, and bent. In 1907 Charles Eliot, the president of Harvard, claimed that Jews were physically inferior and should not be permitted to intermarry. A year later T. A. Bingham, the New York City police commissioner, declared that the nefarious cunning of Jews resulted in their constituting half of the city's criminals.

At the same time, and in addition to the popular basketball programs offered in YMHAs, other Jewish-dominated organizations began to field teams. These included labor unions and socialist groups whose primary motivation was to induce participating players into joining their respective movements.

Of course, there were numerous outstanding Gentile players scattered throughout the country, but most of them were centered in the Northeast. In 1898 these players were sufficient in number to join forces in forming the National Basketball League (NBL), the sport's first professional league. Despite claiming to be "national" in scope, the six charter teams were situated in Philadelphia and neighboring cities in New Jersey. Two years later several other pro leagues started up, including the New York State League, which featured a short-lived franchise in Little Falls, New York. It was here that Paul "Twister" Steinberg became the first known Jewish professional basketball player.

Born in New York City, Steinberg most likely learned the game at a Lower East Side YMHA or community center, but it was on the football field that he enjoyed his most spectacular successes. While playing pro football for several teams, including the Philadelphia Athletics and the Syracuse All-Stars, Steinberg earned his nickname for his elusive running in the open field. Dr. Harry March, celebrated as the "father of pro football," said this about Steinberg: "He ran with what seemed to be a limp combined with a pivot and hip shake which made him a menace to opponents. . . . He was the most elusive, fastest, slickest, shrewdest back of the century."

As for Steinberg, he credited his basketball background for his achievements on the gridiron: "It was natural for me to change directions when in motion with the ball. I adopted the habit from my experience in basketball."

If Steinberg evolved into a celebrated football player, during the first half of the twentieth century, many (if not most) of America's most outstanding and most influential basketballers were Jews, who likewise learned the game in the Lower East Side's ethnic community centers. Foremost among these organizations was the University Settlement House (USH), charted in 1886 by a trio of wealthy Jewish reformers, Stanley Colt, Charles Bunstein Stover, and Carl Schultz, with the aim of helping Jewish immigrants to "understand American ideas." In addition to providing the requisite English-language courses, social clubs, and a library, the University Settlement House also established the first kindergarten and public baths in New York City.

In addition, the gymnasium in the USH became a fertile incubator wherein the first generation of nationally celebrated Jewish basketballers was nurtured. Indeed, early in the twentieth century, the USH was hailed as a "basketball factory." And there's no question that the one individual most responsible for the development of the entire Jewish basketball culture in New York and beyond was a resident staff member at the University Settlement House named Harry Braun.

Born in Austria on July 18, 1882, Braun immigrated to the United States and settled in New York, eventually graduating from the City College of New York (CCNY) in 1902. The only sport he had played was lacrosse, but in 1908 he agreed to do volunteer work at the University Settlement House coaching the youth basketball team. Sometimes called "the midget" team, its roster was composed of players who were not considered tall enough to make their high school varsities. Using the only sport he knew, Braun copied the basics of lacrosse—an up-tempo pace; quick, short passes; and tight man-to-man defenses that featured (for the first time in basketball) the theory and practice of switching. He drove his players hard, insisting that they moved with and without the ball, kept their heads up, and unselfishly looked to pass to an open teammate. His young players proudly called themselves the "Busy Izzies."

During his five years coaching at this level, Braun's teams won five intersettlement championships. Yet despite his success, he refused to coach the USH's more senior teams. His reasoning was that, unlike the older players, the youngsters hadn't had time to develop bad habits and were more eager to accept and learn his precepts. In 1910 he left coaching to devote himself to a career in engineering.

Although Harry Braun's life and deeds have long since been forgotten, and his interest in basketball brief, he deserves recognition as being the originator of fundamental basketball tactics that are still universally employed. Indeed, his game plan was carried on by his pupils, many of whom became the best professional players in the early days of the game. These included Barney Sedran, Marty Friedman, Louis Sugarman, Ira Streusand, Jake and Alex Furstman, and Harry Brill.

Ossie Schectman, who one day would score the very first basket in the Basketball Association of America (BAA, the precursor of the NBA), grew up playing basketball in New York City. He remembers the small gyms and the low ceilings. "You played in a figure-eight and there was lots of movement," he said. "It was devoid of long set shots."

Basketball Hall of Famer Hubie Brown calls this style of play "Jew Ball" and cites it as containing the basic principles that have enabled teams like the San Antonio Spurs, the Los Angeles Lakers, and the Chicago Bulls to win numerous NBA Championships in the modern era.

Testimony: Richie Goldberg

Richie Goldberg was an All-City point guard at James Madison High School in Brooklyn who accepted a basketball scholarship from Mississippi Southern in 1955. "I don't think they'd seen too many Jews down there," he says. "They thought that the Star of David that I wore around my neck was some kind of basketball medal. They also thought my mezuzah was a broken whistle."

The only direct anti-Semitism he encountered was getting booed when he was introduced as a member of the starting lineup before a game at Christian Brothers University in Memphis, Tennessee. But he did overhear a Mississippi Southern coed say this: "If we let Jews into the school, before you know it we'll let niggers in."

2

....

Busy Izzies Take Over

The best of the Busy Izzies and, as far as anybody knows, the best basketball player in the country became the first Jew to achieve stardom in the college game.

Louis Sugarman
5'7", 145 POUNDS

Born in the Bronx in 1890, Louis Sugarman made daily trips to the USH to learn, develop, and master this new game—a game that bore little resemblance to the one played today by sky-walking, slam-dunking, iconic, millionaire, acrobatic giants.

The typical court was about sixty-five feet long and thirty-five feet wide (today's standardized dimensions for college and pros are ninety-four feet by fifty feet). However, since players as tall as six feet were rare and considered freaks, there was ample room for players to maneuver.

If the courts were smaller, the ball was bigger and heavier—a circumference of thirty-two inches and weighing a probable average of about twenty-eight to thirty ounces compared to thirty inches and twenty to twenty-two ounces in modern times. Moreover, the ball that Sugarman and his contemporaries used was made of leather covering a rubber bladder and sealed with raised laces. Because the laces were hand stitched, the actual size, weight, and roundness of the balls were never uniform. The smooth surface made the ball difficult to handle, and if the laces chanced to hit the floor, the dribble or pass (or both) would most likely bounce in an unanticipated direction.

Given all of these handicaps, Sugarman was renowned for his tricky dribbling that—along with his unsurpassed speed and quickness—could easily get past his erstwhile defender and approach the rim. Once he got there, however, Sugarman frequently faced a challenge that's unheard of nowadays, that is, the hoops on many basketball courts lacked a backboard.

Despite these handicaps, Sugarman was only sixteen years old when his ballhandling and scoring prowess landed him a basketball scholarship at Syracuse University. He arrived on the campus with a reputation as a hothead who didn't think twice about physically assaulting opponents. However, Sugarman generally reserved his punches for players on other teams who repeatedly screamed racial epithets at him. Indeed, during a home game pitting Syracuse against Cornell, Jew baiting was the reason Sugarman decked a trio of the visiting players.

In any event, Sugarman single-handedly improved the fortunes of the previously mediocre Syracuse basketball program. The team opened the 1907–8 season with eight consecutive wins. He tallied a game-high seventeen points in a 42–22 win over Rensselaer Polytechnic Institute, followed by a thirteen-point effort as Syracuse beat Williams 25–21. The Orangemen finished with a 10–3 record, by far their best showing since basketball became a varsity sport in 1899.

Then for some reason that has not survived, Sugarman transferred to Notre Dame, where he helped the 1908–9 Irishmen to a record of 33-7. This was the first but certainly not the last time that a Catholic college recruited a Jewish hooper to lead their team to glory.

After two seasons as an undergraduate player, Sugarman became a professional. For the next ten years, he played with several teams in the Eastern League (EL) and the New York State League, where he was the league's leading scorer in 1914.

There were major differences among the early pro leagues. The Eastern League employed backboards and surrounded the courts with wire cages. The cages were designed to keep the more passionate fans from injuring opposing players, but since the ball was never out-of-bounds, the games were extremely physical. Moreover, each team had a designated free-throw shooter who took all of his team's foul shots. The New York State League dispensed with backboards. Instead, the baskets were hung from a rod coming down from the rafters.

Both leagues permitted a two-handed dribble that enabled the player with the ball to aggressively back his defender toward the basket. Fouls were rarely called, and substitutions were not allowed, so if a player suffered an injury, his team played four-on-five.

There were several other pro leagues operating when Sugarman was playing for pay: the Pennsylvania State League, the Connecticut State League, the Interstate League, the Hudson River League, and the Central League. Since there were no interleague agreements, players and teams frequently sold their services to the highest bidder and jumped from league to league. Following the money, the best players would often play in three or even four games a day. But because of the routine franchise shifts and players constantly on the move, fan interest waned and all of these leagues were short-lived. When various teams folded, the players would depart on barnstorming tours.

If playing professional basketball was often a chaotic experience, the average pro earned about twenty-four hundred dollars per season (the equivalent in current value of slightly more than sixty-eight thousand dollars), whereas a skilled laborer made eight hundred dollars annually.

Sugarman's loyalty was unusual, as was his decision in 1917 to quit the game and undertake a new career by enrolling in Philadelphia Dental College. But he couldn't stay away from the game, eventually coaching teams at Penn, Syracuse, and Princeton before occasionally resuming his pro career and then working as a referee.

But Sugarman wasn't the only graduate of the Busy Izzies who made his mark in the pro game.

Ira Streusand

5'6½", 120 POUNDS

Born in Austria, Ira Streusand's parents emigrated to the United States when he was an infant and settled into a crowded apartment on Pitt Street on the Lower East Side of Manhattan.

He described the early days of his basketball career to the authors of *Encyclopedia of Jews in Sports*: "One day, while I was walking past the Clark Settlement House, the director asked me if I was interested in joining a basketball team that played after meetings there. That was in 1901 or 1902 and I subsequently organized the first Jewish boys club at Clark House."

Shortly thereafter, Streusand was recruited by Harry Baum to play with his Busy Izzies at the University Settlement House. "We soon became inter-settlement and AAU [Amateur Athletic Union] midget champs," said Streusand. "As kids, we were all physically inferior. We were real midgets; hardly weighed anything at all. But Baum taught us a new brand of ball and we ran everybody ragged."

Streusand went on to attend Townsend Harris High School before enrolling at CCNY in February 1907. He attended his first class there on a Thursday and two days later played on CCNY's varsity basketball team. "We went to West Point and beat Army 28–23. I scored 22 of City's points."

But throughout his basketball career, Streusand's parents offered little encouragement. "My father was ordained as a rabbi at the age of 17. Although he didn't practice as a rabbi, he felt that education was most important, and that athletics were a waste of time. In deference to his feelings I never discussed my basketball playing at home."

Streusand officially became a professional at the age of fourteen when he was paid five dollars per game for pitching every Sunday for a Municipal League baseball team. "Nobody asked me about my amateur status at CCNY so I didn't volunteer the information. As a matter of fact, all the kids I played with at the University Settlement House were pros by the time they attended college."

While playing for CCNY, Streusand was also getting paid to hoop—eight dollars per game to start with, but eventually earning as much as thirty dollars per. During his rather brief four-year career as a pro, he played for several teams in the New York State, Hudson River, and Eastern Leagues—Catskill, Albany, Syracuse, Kingston, Greystock, and Newburgh (where he led the league in scoring at 12.7 points per game [ppg]). He often played as many as fifteen games every week for different teams in different leagues.

"Pro basketball in those early days was the hardest physical game imaginable," he said. "The chicken wire that enclosed the court was eight feet high," and players would literally throw opponents into the netting, oftentimes drawing blood as their skin was cut by the wires. "I ran into anti-Semitism everywhere, from my first collegiate game until I retired from basketball. I don't know how many times I heard, 'Get the little sheenie.'"

After his sophomore year at CCNY, Streusand yielded to his parents' wishes and enrolled at New York Law School. One year later he made another switch, this time to New York University (NYU), where he played basketball with Joe Girsdansky.

"In those days," Streusand recalled, "all foul shots were taken by one player. But I was so good from the foul line that my Newburgh team easily won the league championship. As a result, a rule was passed that each man who was fouled had to shoot his own foul shots."

Streusand's left the game in 1913 to become a player on Wall Street. The money he had earned playing professionally enabled him to buy a seat on the Stock Exchange and eventually become a millionaire.

Max "Marty" Friedman
5'7", 138 POUNDS

The best defensive guard of his generation, Marty Friedman graduated into the pro ranks after growing too big for the Busy Izzies. Playing with Hudson Company F out of Utica, he teamed with a trio of fellow former Izzies (Barney Sedran, Jack Fox, and William Cohn) to win the New York State Championship in 1914. After defeating the champ of the Eastern League, Friedman and his teammates claimed the title of "world champions." Overall, Friedman played for twenty teams and won six championships in five leagues.

"During most of my career," Friedman said,

> my partner was the great Barney Sedran. We were known as the "Heavenly Twins." We got the name by accident. Barney and I were playing in a couple of different leagues one year and the clubs worked out their schedules to accommodate us. Anyway, an unscrupulous promoter advertised that we were going to play with his team. We weren't supposed to and didn't know about it so we didn't show up. Well, the promoter lied and said that we didn't show because of a schedule conflict that day. The inference was that we preferred with another team even though we were booked with the phony's club. The newspapers picked up the story and called us the "Heavenly Twins." It was meant to be sarcastic and indicated that we could do no wrong. Anyway, the name stuck and the way it eventually was used was completely different from the original intention.

Friedman said about the anti-Semitism he encountered: "I ran into little anti-Semitism among the players of my day. It cropped up mainly in the Midwest among the fans. I guess it was because the Ku Klux Klan was a big power there."

Barney Sedran
5'4", 118 POUNDS

Called the "Mighty Mite," Barney Sedran shortened his surname from Sedransky to try to avoid being another victim of the anti-Semitism that was rampant in America. He attended DeWitt Clinton High School but was not permitted to try out for the varsity team because of his diminutive size. It was at CCNY that Sedran showed himself to be an accomplished scorer and playmaker.

A *New York Evening Post* article said this of his exploits: "Sedran drifting around the court like the ghost of an anemic tubercular, was the sensational midget of a team which defeated Yale, Penn, Princeton, Harvard, Navy, Columbia and Army."

Set shots, free throws, underhand scoops, and hook shots were the standard repertoire, and Sedran mastered them all. The competition was so vicious that even blatant punches were considered to be acceptable defensive techniques. No matter what the shot, even a simple layup, a player's feet never left the floor. Jumping was reserved for rebounding, catching errant passes, and, of course, for jump balls—all situations where an airborne player could reasonably protect himself. But elevating with the ball in hand was "suicide," Sedran said, "because you'd be lucky if you came down alive."

Despite his accomplishments, Sedran was still deemed to be too short to survive in the even rougher ranks of the pros. But Busy Izzy teammate Marty Friedman got him a tryout with Utica in the New York State League, and Sedran became one of the best pay-for-play "basketballers" of his time. As was the norm at the time, Sedran played for several teams in several different leagues—competing in as many as three games per day. No wonder he earned as much as $12,000 annually (the equivalent of nearly $280,000 in 2015).

Allie McWilliams matched up against Sedran many times and offered this scouting report: "Guarding him was like playing a mosquito. You'd be lucky to see where he was, and if you tried to move in on him, you'd hear a buzz. That's how you could tell he dribbled by."

Into the 1920s fragile, short-lived new pro leagues came into being, old ones folded, and barely surviving leagues played musical franchises. Sedran joined many of his fellow pros in forming barnstorming teams. Among the more notable of these were the Brooklyn Dux, which means "leader" in Latin. The three-letter name was also chosen to keep down the cost of team jerseys. Included in the fifty-cent admission, a dance was held after every game. Also notable were the Hebrew Cyclones, the House of David, and the Jersey City Hebrews, which featured future baseball star Hank Greenberg in the midtwenties.

According to Nat Holman, Sedran "was the greatest little man who ever played the game. He could do everything. A great outside and inside shooter, smart passer, great ball handler, and very fast. He was always in motion, setting up play situations which resulted in baskets. He used his mind at all times and for a little man withstood the punishment that was characteristic of the rough and tumble contact game in the early days of the sport. He was the most complete player of his time. He was afraid of none and dared all."

Other noteworthy former Izzies include Harry Brill and Jake Fuller, who both played at CCNY, and in 1912 teamed with Friedman and Sedran as Newburgh won the Hudson River League Championship.

Testimony: David Blatt

David Blatt played his college ball at Princeton and went on to coach professional teams in Greece, Italy, Israel, and Turkey and also led Russia to a bronze medal in the 2012 Olympic Games. Starting in the 2014–15 season, Blatt coached the Cleveland Cavaliers.

"Coaching in Turkey was my least pleasant experience," he says. "There was no overt anti-Semitism directed at me, but it was always there under the surface. That's why I never felt safe there."

Indeed, the only direct incident came in Naples in southern Italy. "We won a game that knocked the local team out of contention," Blatt recalls, "and the fans stormed out of the stands to attack us. One guy got into my face and started screaming in Italian, a language that I knew. 'You shitty Jew!' he yelled. One of my players pulled me away."

3

....

Beyond the Izzies

There were many important non-Izzies in the first two decades of the twentieth century.

Henry Elias was born in New York and, in 1901, as a member of Columbia University's initial basketball team, became the first Jewish player there. After graduating Elias accepted a nonpaying position as Columbia's coach, guiding the team to a composite record of 36-2 and back-to-back national championships in 1904 and 1905.

Another native New Yorker, Harry Fisher was the star of Elias's championship teams. On March 10, 1905, he set a Columbia record by scoring thirteen field goals, a mark that wouldn't be surpassed for forty-eight years. Fisher was a two-year All-American before succeeding Elias and becoming the Lions' first paid coach.

During the 1909–10 season Fisher did double-duty—coaching both Columbia and St. John's. This was, and continues to be, a unique situation. (There's no evidence that the two teams played each other that season.) In 1921 he became the head basketball coach at West Point.

Fisher's lifetime coaching records include 101-39 at Columbia, 15-5 at St. John's, and 46-5 during his three years at West Point.

In addition, in 1905 Fisher was named to a four-person committee that was charged with writing the first college basketball rules. He then became the first editor of the newly formed *Collegiate Rules Committee and Collegiate Guide*, a position he held until 1915.

In 1907 Joseph "Gid" Girsdansky became a member of NYU's first basketball team and three years later was named the team's first Jewish captain. Playing under the name Joe Gordon, he was a member of the Newburgh team that won the Hudson River League title in 1912.

Joe Weiner was born in New Haven, Connecticut, and became the first Jew to play for Yale. In 1915 he led the Bulldogs to the Ivy League title and was voted one of the five best players in the league.

He later starred on an all-Jewish barnstorming team, the Atlas Basketball Team, which toured through Connecticut and Massachusetts.

Frank Basloe was born in Hungary in 1887 and was a young child when his family immigrated to Herkimer, New York. As with most young-sters from impoverished families, Basloe learned the game with a ball made of rags that he tossed into a wooden barrel hoop. Described as a sometime basketball player, vaudeville comedian who performed with W. C. Fields and Buster Keaton, and promoter of marathon runs, motorcycle races, and prizefights, Basloe's most noteworthy accomplishment was organizing and promoting basketball teams.

In 1903 Basloe was only sixteen years old when he organized, managed, promoted, and played for a professional team in Herkimer that earned the impressive amount of $300 (the equivalent of $7,742 today) for the season. Flushed with his initial success, Basloe fielded pro teams for the next twenty years.

In 1911 he promoted the 31st Separate Company team of Her-kimer. In the fall of that year Basloe's outfit went up against the Buffalo Germans, considered to be the most potent ball club extant. Indeed, during the 1904 Olympic Games, basketball was introduced as "a demonstration sport." The Germans were undefeated in the minitournament, outscoring opponents by 238–70. Moreover, the

Germans were riding a 110-game winning streak—but were beaten by Basloe's ball club. To prove that the victory was no fluke, various editions of Basloe's teams defeated the mighty Germans four of the subsequent five games they met.

In 1914 another of Basloe's squads—the Globe Trotters—became the first basketball team to undertake a cross-country tour. Over the course of his entrepreneurial endeavors, his teams traveled nearly one hundred thousand miles and compiled a record of 1,324–127.

After his touring days were done, Basloe owned teams in the New York State League and was president of the league from 1937 to 1941 and, after play resumed after World War II, in 1947–48.

If the man who was celebrated as "basketball's first ambassador" has been mostly forgotten, the library in Herkimer is named after him.

During the first quarter of the twentieth century, there were several other noteworthy Jewish players who did not learn the game in the University Settlement House.

Maclun "Mac" Baker played for NYU and was the first Jew ever named to both the collegiate All-America and AAU All-America teams.

Samuel Meltzer was known as a great dribbler during his standout career at Columbia. The only outbreak of anti-Semitism he encountered was when Columbia made a tour of the South during Christmas week in 1908. "Occasionally somebody would shout, 'Get the Jew,' but I never let it bother me."

Michael Saxe played at the University of Pennsylvania and then coached the first basketball team fielded by Villanova University, a Catholic institution. For many years the Michael Saxe Memorial Trophy was awarded to the most outstanding college player in Philadelphia.

Al Tisch (né Tischinsky) was the only Caucasian who played with the All-Negro Renaissance teams.

Testimony: Neal Walk

Neal Walk had an eight-year NBA career with Phoenix, New Orleans, and New York. But the only anti-Semitism he encountered was as a high school student.

Neal's father was a salesman who moved the family from Cleveland to Miami Beach when Neal was six. His parents conversed in Yiddish when they didn't want Neal to understand what they were saying.

The kids attending Miami Beach High School drove there in Corvettes and Rolls-Royces, and the student population was "99.9 percent Jewish."

Neal and his teammates faced anti-Semitism during most road games. "There'd be fans dressed in overalls and chewing stalks of straw," he said, "and throw bagels and coins at us. Then we'd smirk as we'd beat the shit out of whatever team we were playing.

"Hey, we were the Chosen People. The Jews triumphant over the infidel rednecks. Those were probably the most satisfying wins of my entire career."

4

....

Enter Sir Nat

Kareem Abdul-Jabbar hails from the New York metropolitan area. So does Julius Erving. Yet in 1976 an official proclamation from the Boys' Athletic League named Nat Holman as the greatest basketball product to come out of the city. There is no question that Nat Holman was an authentic founding father. A friend said of Holman, "Sometimes Nat acted as though he was sore that Dr. Naismith beat him to the punch."

Nat Holman was born in New York City on October 19, 1896, the fourth of ten children of Russian immigrant parents. Papa was a hard worker and soon saved enough to buy a small grocery store on Norfolk Street. With seven sons, help was cheap and dependable. The Holman boys all followed the same routine. They awoke before the sun to open, clean, and stock the store. They stayed up late cleaning and replenishing the shelves. But Papa also insisted on the virtues of a formal education, making sure that the boys all did their homework. In a time when a high school diploma was a rarity, all seven of the Holman boys went to college.

It was a crowded, busy household, and sometimes the growing boys got into each other's way. They heatedly competed for attention and survival, but they didn't dare compete with Papa's iron hand. One after another, all seven brothers turned their spirited natures to sports.

Basketball was their favorite game, and their first collective basketball was an old vegetable sack stuffed with paper. But the brothers Holman were all-around athletes. Irving played high school basketball. Jack and Arthur played high school soccer. Morris captained the CCNY basketball team in 1918. Aaron played on the NYU basketball team that won the AAU Championship in 1920. Sandy also played basketball at NYU.

"I was first attracted to basketball in Seward Park," said Holman. "An instructor at the playground there really got me going at the age of ten. Then there was the Educational Alliance and the Henry Street Settlement."

A BROTHER REMEMBERS: "We all played basketball and were good. But Nat was the ace."

At twelve Nat was playing against grown men as a substitute for the team that represented the Henry Street Settlement. The tiny court left an indelible mark on his basketball philosophy. The playing area measured seventy feet by forty feet, and any player foolish enough to take off in a burst of straightaway speed was in imminent danger of splattering himself against a wall. Defense consisted of a five-man barrier standing from sideline to sideline. In such cramped quarters goals could be earned only by jockeying and weaving, by acquiring a relentless repertoire of subtle and deceptive movements. Nat Holman was the most artful dodger of them all.

Nat entered the High School of Commerce in 1912, playing basketball, baseball, and football and being named to the all-city soccer team. He then matriculated at the Savage School for Physical Education. While there he also launched his pro career with the Knickerbocker Big Five. He was five foot eleven and 165 pounds and was paid five dollars a game.

It was common for the best collegiate basketball players in and around New York to pick up a few surreptitious dollars by playing under assumed names for pro teams on weekends. Questions of amateurism and eligibility were totally ignored: there were several instances where an undergraduate who was enrolled in one school would play in an intercollegiate game for a different school.

In 1919 Holman turned down a professional baseball contract offered by the Cincinnati Reds, choosing instead to accept an offer from CCNY to teach hygiene as well as to coach soccer and freshman basketball.

After a one-year stint in the U.S. Navy at the tail end of World War I, Holman was named the head coach of the CCNY varsity basketball team (succeeding Dr. Leonard Palmer, another Jew). Holman was the youngest college coach in the country, and he augmented his salary by playing for pay with Germantown and leading the Eastern League in scoring in 1921.

Virtually all of the pro games were played inside either a chicken-wire or a rope netting, an environment that required a special set of skills. Holman explained:

> For instance, a man would go under the basket, take a shot, and relax as he went into the netting that surrounded the court. The trailer following the first man down the court had to know just how to fade out of the way before the man bounced back from the netting and smashed into him.

> When chicken wire was used to enclose a court instead of rope netting, the game was even rougher. I wore the heaviest pads I could get. It got so bad that one sporting goods company designed special metal reinforced trunks to protect the players. To keep the wire from giving way, there were two-by-four timbers around the court. It was a common practice to hit an opponent hard and drive him into the boards to slow him down. We would also throw bounce-passes off the wire like in racquetball.

> Then with the cage shaking and the floor swaying and the fans in the gallery tossing peanuts and pop bottles and their language searing you on both sides, you would step up and try to shoot a foul.

> I experienced no anti-Semitism from my opponents during my pro career. Occasionally there would be some nasty remarks from the sideline. But on the whole I had very little of it.

In 1921 while Holman was coaching CCNY and playing with Germantown, two dominant pro teams evolved in New York: the Whirlwinds and the Celtics. The former ball club was a mostly Jewish outfit that featured Chris Leonard, Barney Sedran, and Marty Friedman. The latter was composed of a bunch of tough Irish kids from the neighborhood around Twenty-Third Street and Ninth Avenue. Both teams made substantial bids for Holman's services, but he chose the Whirlwinds.

It was inevitable that these two ball clubs would meet, so a three-game series was arranged to determine the unofficial champion of the metropolitan area. The first game was played on April 11, 1921, and drew eleven thousand fans to the Seventy-First Regiment Armory. The rules of the amateur game were in effect, which eliminated double dribbling and encouraged the referees to call fouls on the slightest physical contact. As a result, a total of fifty-three fouls were called over the course of the forty-minute contest.

The amateur rules still permitted one player to shoot all of the free throws awarded to his team. Holman scored all of his team-leading twenty-two points from the foul line, while Johnny Beckman recorded one basket and twenty-three free throws for the Celtics.

The Whirlwinds prevailed, 40-27.

The second game was played at the Sixty-Ninth Regiment Armory before a crowd of eight thousand. This game was conducted under pro rules, which made the play more physical than the initial one. Accordingly, fewer fouls were called, and the Celtics won a seesaw battle, 26-24.

The third game was not played. According to the *Reach Guide*, the reason for the cancellation was that "certain gamblers" attempted to bribe certain players to deliberately lose the deciding game.

The real reason appears to have been that the Celtics offered Holman and Leonard large sums of money to switch uniforms. It was said that Holman agreed to switch teams and agreed to a payday of $2,000 per month ($24,207 in 2015) for playing in two games every week—including the rubber game of the Whirlwind-Celtics miniseries.

And, indeed, both Holman and Leonard subsequently played for the Celtics for several years thereafter.

Holman was a great passer, an excellent shooter, and a clever improviser. He was responsible for having the Celtics' biggest player (Dutch Dehnert) position himself in the "pivot," close to the basket with his back to the hoop. This allowed the Celtics to create a picking, cutting give-and-go offense.

Holman was the smallest player on the team but the most dynamic. His self-assured style of play could be counted on to rile up an already hostile crowd. There were many times when Holman had to concentrate on the game while simultaneously trying to avoid being jabbed with hat pins or scalded with burning cigars by irate courtside spectators.

Holman was joined on the Celtics by another outstanding Jewish player, Marty Banks, in 1925, but Nat was the game's biggest draw. From 1920 to 1928 the Celtics won 720 of 795 games.

AN OLD PRO REMEMBERS: Nat had talent, flair, intelligence, and an unquenchable arrogance. He spoke with a phony British accent, and his sentences were always laced with literary references. The customers would pay to see Nat fall on his face, but they were always disappointed. Nat Holman was to basketball as Babe Ruth, Red Grange, Jack Dempsey, and Bill Tilden were to their sports. But being a professional basketball player was a difficult way to make a living. We played about a hundred games a year. We'd play Friday night and beat the yokels by a narrow margin. Then we'd get some bets down, play them again on Sunday afternoon, and kill them. We'd collect our money and get the hell out of town. The Celtics were doing the same kind of thing when Nat was playing with them. Only we didn't call it point shaving. We called it survival.

Holman quit playing in 1930 and coached CCNY with the same energy, arrogance, and enthusiasm he exhibited as a player. He drove his college players—who were almost exclusively Jews—with an insistence on perfection that bordered on ruthlessness and turned out winners year after year.

Testimony: Nancy Lieberman

Nancy Lieberman was born in Brooklyn on July 1, 1958, and grew up to become the best women's hooper ever. "We moved to Far Rockaway in Queens when I was an infant," she says. "It was a Jewish neighborhood, and my parents' religious practices were very strict. We kept a kosher home and regularly went to *shule*."

As soon as she was able to dribble a basketball, Lieberman realized that she had found what she wanted to do with her life. "But the Jewish people in the neighborhood were very judgmental," she recalls. "Why was I always playing in the park? And playing with black guys? Why couldn't I act more like a girl?"

In 1976 while still a student at Far Rockaway High School, Lieberman was named to the USA women's basketball squad that won a silver medal in the Montreal Olympics. "My mom really didn't want me to go to Montreal," Lieberman says. "She was afraid that something like the massacre of Israeli athletes that happened in Munich four years before might happen again. She wanted me to change my name to Lieb, so I wouldn't be identified as a Jew. But, of course, I refused."

Next for Lieberman was achieving All-American status at Old Dominion University in Norfolk, Virginia. That's where her incredible passing earned her a nickname—"Lady Magic"—but she was also a record-setting scorer, rebounder, and free-throw shooter. "There was a large Jewish population in Norfolk," she says, "so I felt comfortable there and was invited to many seder dinners. I was always proud of being a Jew. There aren't a lot of us in sports, so I've always tried to represent myself correctly."

After playing in several other international tournaments, Lieberman continued her career in a men's professional league—the United States Basketball League. Also on her résumé are stints in the short-lived Women's Pro Basketball League and with the Washington Generals, the perpetual patsies for the Harlem Globetrotters.

At age thirty-nine Lieberman concluded her active career in 1997, with the Phoenix Mercury in the Women's National Basketball Association's inaugural season. The following season she was hired as the head coach and general manager of the WNBA's Detroit Shock. Three years later she left the Shock to work as a women's basketball analyst on ESPN. Then on July 24, 2008, the fifty-year-old Lieberman signed a contract with the Shock and played in one game—registering two assists in a losing effort versus the Houston Comets. She is somewhat wistful that the WNBA didn't exist during her prime. "I would have loved it," she admits, "but I never really worry about what I never had. You are what you are."

In November 2009 Lieberman added to her credentials as a pioneer, becoming the head coach of the Texas Legends in the NBA Development League, an affiliate of the Dallas Mavericks—thereby becoming the first woman to coach a professional men's basketball team. She later moved to a front-office position with the Legends before becoming an analyst for *Thunder Live*, a pre- and postgame studio show on Fox Sports Oklahoma.

Then in July 2015 she joined the Sacramento Kings as an assistant coach, becoming the second female assist coach in NBA history. (San Antonio's Becky Hammon preceded Lieberman in 2014.) "Like all the other assistants in the league," she notes, "I have several teams that I'm responsible for scouting, and my area of specialization is scouting player personnel. Being Jewish has no impact on my job. I'm seen more as a woman than a Jew."

Because of the Kings' poor performance early in the 2015–16 season, there were persistent rumors that head coach George Karl would be fired—with Lieberman proposed in some sources as possibly replacing him. But Lieberman scoffed at any suggestion that Karl was in any way an inferior coach. "George is amazing," she said. "He knows more about the game than anybody I've ever met. And he knows how to teach what he knows." When Karl was indeed fired at the conclusion of the 2015–16 season, Lieberman was retained as one of the Kings' assistants.

Lieberman believes that it's only a matter of time and circumstance before a woman is hired to be the head coach of an NBA team. "Carly Fiorina and Hillary Clinton are currently running to be president of the United States," she says. "Besides, women have always been telling men what to do, whether as grandmother, mother, or wife."

Looking back, has Lieberman ever been the target of anti-Semitism? "Never," she stated. "Even at a young age, I got so much attention for my game that I was always treated with respect. When I became an Olympian, some of that respect turned to reverence. But none of that ever turned my head. I was what I was, and I am what I am. Just trying to do the right thing under any and every circumstance. Which, when you come down to it, really has nothing to do with being Jewish."

5

....

Gotty and the SPAHS

Born in New York City in 1899, Eddie Gottlieb grew up with an unbridled enthusiasm for whatever sport happened to be in season. "I was only a little shaver," he recalled, "and I would hitch rides on the back of ice trucks to go watch the New York Giants play in the Polo Grounds."

The family moved to Philadelphia when he was nine years old, and in 1913 he entered South Philadelphia High School, where he played varsity football and basketball as well as junior varsity baseball. "There were only two things I couldn't do in baseball," he said, "hit and throw. I was quarterback on the football team only because I was the only guy who could remember the signals." If his athletic ability lacked distinction, Gottlieb demonstrated a keen mind for numbers and could work out complex mathematical problems without using pencil and paper.

Upon his graduation in 1916, Gottlieb's next stops were the Philadelphia School of Pedagogy (where he once scored twenty-six points in an intramural basketball game) and then Temple University. With his degrees in hand, Gottlieb taught physical education at a local elementary school for three years before moving on to become a sporting-goods salesman.

Still, he considered these jobs to be only way stations while he pursued his primary ambition—to play and coach basketball. In the process he played anywhere for any team that would have him. And because he spoke with such confidence about bounce passes, back-door cuts, and one-footed changes of direction, he was often allowed to coach.

As a hedge against the stark necessities of having to live in the real world, Gottlieb also got involved with promoting as many sporting events in as many venues as possible—wrestling, boxing, and the like—such as various armories and dance halls around town, "because," he said, "that's where the money was."

Gottlieb's dreams began coming true in 1918, when Harry Passon and Hughie Black joined him in organizing the South Philadelphia Hebrew Association basketball team, nicknamed the SPAHS. Players on that original SPAHS team sometimes included Nat Holman, Barney Sedran, and Marty Friedman, with Passon a fixture and Gottlieb himself serving also as the team's coach.

The front of their uniforms bore the Hebrew letters *samach*, *pey*, *hey*, and *aleph*, which spelled out "SPAHS." For road games, the back of their jerseys reminded spectators that they were "Hebrews." The players earned five dollars per game, the modern-day equivalent of eighty dollars. Under Gottlieb's passionate guidance, and throughout the team's long, glorious history, the vast majority of the SPAHS were Jewish.

Gottlieb was the player-coach until 1925, when a hand injury forced him to retire to the bench. "That's also when I quit my job at the sporting-goods store," Gottlieb said, "and devoted myself full-time to coaching the SPAHS."

A lifelong bachelor, Gottlieb was married to basketball. He was rather corpulent, measuring five foot eight and 220 pounds, and he tried to enliven his sad eyes and pasty skin by always wearing bright-red bow ties.

In those early days many basketball teams tried to survive as the prelude to dances. For the SPAHS the scene of many of these double features was the grand ballroom of the Broadwood Hotel, where the admission was sixty-five cents for men and thirty-five cents for women. The SPAHS would play at eight thirty, and the women would be allowed into the ballroom for the dance at eleven. Even as he coached the team, Gottlieb would simultaneously count the house.

"Many Jewish people wouldn't let their daughters go to an ordinary dance," Gottlieb said, "except when the SPAHS were the opening event. I remember one of my players, Gil Fitch, getting out of his uniform after the third quarter and, not having enough time for a shower, he put on a suit, climbed onto the stage, and led his band to kick off the dancing. Kitty Kallen got her start singing with Fitch's band."

Gottlieb was always trying different ways to draw crowds. One of his brainstorms was to have his publicity man, Dave Zinkoff, compose, print, and distribute a free numbered program for each game. "There'd be a gossip column," Zinkoff recalled. "Who was dancing with whom. The players were listed, and so was the playlist for that night's dance. The back pages featured a big ad for one of Philadelphia's most popular men's clothing stores, and for every game, a lucky number was picked, with the winner getting a free nineteen-dollar suit from the store. One guy was so happy when his number came up that he ran over to me and said that with his new suit, he could now get married."

Sometimes the SPAHS played at the YMHA at Broad and Pine Streets, where they would attract crowds in excess of fifteen hundred. With more money at his disposal, Gottlieb began to successfully recruit players from New York City—the likes of Joel "Shikey" Gotthoffer, Red Wolf, and Moe Goldman. And as the team became more formidable, it captivated the attention and admiration of the local Jewish community.

According to SPAHS veteran Harry Litwack, "Every Jewish boy in Philadelphia was playing basketball. Some of them with old laundry baskets nailed to telephone poles and using rags tied together for a ball. And every one of them dreamed of playing for the SPAHS." Indeed, among the large Jewish population of Philadelphia, the SPAHS were far more popular than the city's two major-league baseball teams—the Phillies and the Athletics.

Travel was costly, so although they did occasionally travel to the Midwest, the SPAHS' main rivals were in New York: another Jewish team called the Hakoahs, whose roster was sometimes augmented by Holman; the Celtics, which eventually became Holman's only employer; and the Knights of St. Anthony, which represented the mixed Italian and Jewish neighborhood of Greenpoint in Brooklyn. Wherever they played, Litwack noted, "Half the fans would come to see the Jews get killed, and the other half were Jews coming to see us win."

When the SPAHS played in Brooklyn's Prospect Hall, security guards were hired to search all of the paying customers at the entrance and routinely confiscated significant numbers of guns. But Litwack remembered this venue as still being incredibly dangerous: "They used to have a balcony that hung over the court, and the fans up there would bring sandwiches and bottled beer to the games. Whenever something would happen down on the court that those Brooklyn fans didn't like, they'd send those bottles down on us. There was also a lady in the front row who used to jab us with long hat pins when we ran by."

Even worse were the unexpected stings from the hot pennies that were aimed at the SPAHS. Insults from hostile fans—"Christ killers," "Kikes"—also gave the SPAHS constant reminders that they were playing not only to win but also to gain respect for Jews all over the world.

For the 1922–23 and 1923–24 seasons, the SPAHS were accepted into the short-lived Philadelphia League—and won championships in both of those seasons.

One of the highlights of the first decade of the SPAHS occurred in 1926 when, led by Holman and the Heavenly Twins, they defeated the Celtics and the all-black New York Renaissance in a two-week period.

Until the SPAHS moved into the neophyte Basketball Association of America as the Philadelphia Warriors, the various editions of the team won twelve championships in three different leagues—the aforementioned Philadelphia League, the Eastern League, and the American Basketball League (ABL).

However, even after the SPAHS qua SPAHS were defunct, as we shall see, Eddie Gottlieb's fame and influence reached more elevated heights.

Testimony: Amare Stoudemire

Amare Stoudemire is an African American born in Lake Wales, Florida, and has been an NBA player since 2002. "My parents were both spiritual people," he says. And he was brought up to believe in what he calls "the entire Bible," with the Old Testament offering as many moral and ethical lessons and advice as the New Testament. "I believe," he says, "that Jesus is the Messiah. And a lot of Jewish people don't believe that. But then there are some that do."

Although he has discovered no distinct evidence that any of his mother's ancestors were Jews, Stoudemire says this: "I have been aware since my youth that I have been a Hebrew through my mother's side." His mother's somewhat vague recollections were sufficient for Stoudemire to immerse himself in Judaic history and culture. "I'm not technically Jewish," he says, "but I'm culturally Jewish. It happened organically."

The culture has influenced Stoudemire to the point where he wore a yarmulke and prayer shawl for his 2012 religious wedding. He also engages in Sabbath family dinners and observances of the Jewish holidays. He tweets "Shabbat Shalom" on the eve of the Sabbath and has started days with Twitter messages of "Boker tov," Hebrew for "Good morning." And although the practice is frowned upon in virtually every Judaic practice, Stoudemire has the Star of David tattooed on his shoulder.

The Jewish holidays are a vital factor in Stoudemire's life. "Passover," he says, "is a very important time of the year for my family, only because it puts you under the covenant of God. When you are under the covenant, then you have more of an openness for your prayers. . . . Passover is definitely one of my favorite holy days."

One year when Stoudemire played for the Phoenix Suns, the Day of Atonement happened to fall in the middle of the preseason training camp. Even though the Suns' schedule included two strenuous practices every day, this is what Stoudemire posted on Instagram: "From sundown tonight to sundown tomorrow! No eating or drinking!"

In 2010 Stoudemire made his first visit to Israel, prompting him to initiate the process of attaining Israeli citizenship. That's also when he became a part-owner of Hapoel Jerusalem, an Israeli basketball team.

His next trip to the Holy Land came in the summer of 2013, when he served as an assistant coach to the basketball team that represented Canada at the Maccabiah Games. It was then that Stoudemire also met, and became "best friends" with, Shimon Peres, who was Israel's president.

There have been persistent rumors that Stoudemire would move to Israel and play for their national team once his NBA career was over. "It's entirely possible," he said. "To live, play basketball, and continue my study of Jewish history and culture . . . that's something I'd like to do." This possibility was actualized in 2016 when Stoudemire suited up for Hapoel.

He's also eager to share exactly how his connection to Judaism has benefited him. "From day to day," he say, "both consciously and subconsciously, it's given me a better outlook on life. It's kept me hopeful on so many levels, and it's especially helpful in enabling me to persevere in the face of whatever difficulties I experience and whatever difficulties people everywhere are experiencing. To have shalom, to have peace among all people, that's the proper way to live. It keeps you humble."

6

Taking over the Game

In the late 1890s Joseph Weiner became the first Jew to play on Yale's varsity basketball team. It wasn't until 1922 that another Jew was allowed to succeed Weiner. His name was Sam Pite, but he quit the team midway through the season after Yale's anti-Semitic coach mostly kept him on the bench. However, after Yale finished last in the Ivy League, and after they lost to the Atlas Club, a predominantly Jewish team in New Haven, the coach was fired.

The new coach was Joe Fogarty, who was interested only in winning and couldn't care less about a player's ethnicity. Still, Pite was playing with the Atlas Club and had no intention of returning to Yale. Only when Fogarty came to his house and begged him to reconsider did Pite change his mind. And, of course, Yale won the Ivy League Championship in 1923, and Pite was an all-league selection.

Here's what legendary sportswriter Walter Camp had to say about Pite: "A brilliant Yale forward, Pite is one of the most amazing basketball players I have ever seen in action. He has speed and basketball sense, but more important still, he seems to have an instinctive sense of direction and distance in tossing the ball. This enables him to throw baskets from any section of the floor and from almost any position. He never needs even a second to 'set' himself for a winning toss."

Pite also had the ability to maintain any lead by dribbling the ball all over the court, thereby preventing Yale's opponents from gaining possession. It is said that Pite's elusive ballhandling was instrumental in the establishment of the midcourt time line.

Meanwhile, college basketball was rapidly becoming a major sport. In 1915, 195 colleges fielded basketball teams. By 1922 that number swelled to 440. When Sam Pite was a senior at Yale (1924), six of the Ivy League's top scorers were Jews. Two years later the unofficial metropolitan-area championship was contested between CCNY and NYU. All of CCNY's starters were Jews, as were two of NYU's starters. This was no surprise for two reasons: during Nat Holman's first twelve years coaching CCNY, the Beavers dominated East Coast basketball with a total record of 118-41. And virtually all of the players on each of these teams—including every captain—were Jewish.

Even so, many of New York's Jewish newspapers did not deign to print the scores of collegiate basketball games. The sports pages of the *New York Daily Mirror*, however, occasionally printed scores, summaries of games, and notes on outstanding Jewish players in Yiddish.

As the 1930s dawned, however, the college game became big news—too big for any newspaper in New York and the rest of the country to ignore. And Jewish players became even more dominant and newsworthy than ever before.

Indeed, the most significant example of just how much the Jews so profoundly influenced collegiate basketball was the astounding success of the St. John's Wonder Five. A Roman Catholic school, all of the classrooms on the Brooklyn campus of St. John's University featured a crucifix attached to the front wall. Yet if the Prince of Peace ruled the roost, basketball was the newest testament. That's why St. John's first began recruiting Jewish players in the mid-1920s. This game plan reached its epitome in 1928 when several outstanding Jews enrolled in St. John's.

Max Posnack was born in Brooklyn (date unknown) and attended Thomas Jefferson High School. He played forward and excelled in passing and dribbling.

Mac Kinsbrunner was born in Austria in 1909 and was a young child when his parents immigrated to the United States. After graduating high school in New York City, Kinsbrunner enrolled at Syracuse University but soon transferred to St. John's. According to Red Auerbach and Nat Holman, Kinsbrunner was the greatest dribbler either of them had ever seen.

If the place and date of Allie Schuckman's birth are unknown, it's certain that he was a teammate of Posnack's at Thomas Jefferson High School in Brooklyn and transferred to St. John's after a brief stint at Long Island University (LIU). Schuckman was the Wonder Five's best set shooter and go-to scorer.

Jack "Rip" Gerson was born in New York (date unknown). He was an outstanding player at Commerce High School and then completed a two-year course at the Brooklyn College of Pharmacy, where he also excelled on the basketball court. Unwilling to quit the game, Gerson enrolled at St. John's with the sole purpose of continuing to play. His primary role with the Wonder Five was to play suffocating defense against the opponent's best point maker.

Matty Begovich was born and raised in Hoboken, New Jersey, to refugees from Poland and was the only Gentile among the starters. The rules then in effect called for a jump ball after every score, and at six foot five Begovich controlled the tip far more often than not.

Two other non-Jews played significant roles: Tom Neary, the only important substitute, and James "Buck" Freeman, the varsity coach. Freeman had been a star at St. John's from 1923 to 1927, averaging 7.4 points per game, an impressive achievement back when teams rarely scored more than 30.

As coach of the Wonder Five, Freeman resurrected Harry Baum's innovations in emphasizing quick, clever passing, the give-and-go, and switching on defense. Freeman was also a confirmed bachelor, a night owl, and a hard drinker. By 1937 Freeman's losing battle with the bottle cost him his job.

Back then the game clock ran for forty minutes and wasn't stopped for free throws, out-of-bounds plays, or center jumps. Because there was no midcourt line or shot clock, teams of that era would often run endless weaves on offense until a good shot turned up. And ball clubs would routinely freeze the ball to retain leads.

The Wonder Five were masters at playing this type of slow, conservative, deliberate style—oftentimes working the ball for as long as ten minutes before attempting a shot. And the dribbling ability of Posnack and Kinsbrunner made even the smallest lead a safe one.

If their game plan was certainly boring, their astounding successes were not. Over the course of their three varsity seasons (1928–31), the Wonder Five compiled a record of 68-4.

In the 1928–29 season, the Wonder Five lost an early-season game to Providence, another Catholic school whose best player was Ed Wineapple, a Jewish All-American. But the St. John's Indians won their next eighteen games and finished the season at 23-2.

Their record in the following campaign was 24-1, during which they held opponents to fewer than twenty-one points per game. In 1930–31, during the depths of the Depression, the Wonder Five participated in a historic triple-header organized to benefit New York City's Unemployment Relief Fund. More than fifteen thousand fans were on hand to witness the first college games ever played in Madison Square Garden (MSG). Six local teams were on the card—St. John's, CCNY, NYU, Columbia, Fordham, and Manhattan. The featured game pitted the Wonder Five against CCNY.

City College tallied the first basket of the game, but the combination of the adhesive defense of St. John's and playing keep-away for ten and fifteen minutes at a time prevented CCNY from scoring another field goal until the final minute of the contest. The Wonder Five prevailed 17-9 on their way to a twenty-four-game winning streak. They lost a subsequent game to NYU before winning their last eight games to finish the season at 21-1.

However, two weeks after season's end, news broke that all the members of the Wonder Five (as well as several players from other New York City colleges) had used aliases to play pro ball during their entire undergraduate careers. Although they all denied the charges (which later proved to be unarguably true), all those involved were forced to forfeit their amateur status.

As a group the St. John's players immediately turned pro, calling themselves the Brooklyn Jewels. Two more Jewish played were added to their roster—George Slott and Jack Poliskin—and they barnstormed for two years. In 1933 they changed their name to the New York Jewels and joined the American Basketball League, the most competitive professional circuit in the East. They won two ABL championships (1935 and 1938) before breaking up in 1939 to pursue off-court careers. Even with the disbanding of the Jewels, Jewish cagers continued to dominate both the college and the professional games.

Testimony: Mark Cuban

Mark Cuban is a certified multibillionaire who, in 2000, bought the Dallas Mavericks for a mere $285 million. He originally made his fortune by engaging in several enterprises—from social software to distributing movies. Always a flamboyant character, he's been fined by the NBA a total of at least $1,665,000 for criticizing the league's referees and baiting opposing players. In 2012 he offered to donate $1 million to charity if Donald Trump shaved his head.

His Russian-born grandfather changed the family's name from Chabenisky to Cuban when they passed through Ellis Island early in the twentieth century. When pressed Cuban identifies himself as "a non-practicing Jew," yet this is how one of his representatives responded to an interview request for this book: "Mr. Cuban does not want to talk about that subject."

7

....

The Barnum of Basketball

Abe Saperstein was born in London on July 4, 1901, and along with his family came to America five years later. He grew up in a tough Irish neighborhood in Chicago, where he played baseball and basketball. Despite being only five foot five and not an outstanding athlete, Saperstein's hustle and aggressiveness on the basketball hardwoods were sufficient to earn him five dollars a game playing for the semipro Chicago Reds from 1920 to 1926.

Even though Saperstein wasn't much of a player, he yearned to either find or create a profitable career somehow connected with the game he loved. An opportunity became available in 1927, when Saperstein gained control of an all-black team that was struggling to survive in the highly competitive world of professional basketball.

Giles Post was the name of a team that was founded at the all-black Wendell Phillips High School in 1926 and was playing in the Negro American Legion League, a loose organization of amateur ball clubs. The players readily bought into Saperstein's idea that they could all make a living by turning pro.

His first move was to approach the owners of a new dance hall, the Savoy Ballroom, and make a deal. The owners, looking for some kind of attraction that would attract customers for after-game dances, agreed to sponsor the renamed Savoy Big Five, who would play against a variety of other local teams. But if the association between the SPAHS and the Broadwood Hotel in Philadelphia was a resounding success, the Savoy Big Five was a dismal failure.

Saperstein was not discouraged. He instituted still another name change—Saperstein's Harlem, New York, Globetrotters—and took the team on the road. Saperstein bought a battered 1919 Model T Ford from a funeral director and drove thirty-three miles to the small town of Hinckley, Illinois, for their initial paying gig—easily earning seventy-five dollars for annihilating a squad of local heroes. They were now full-fledged pros.

Saperstein was the chauffeur, coach, trainer, promoter, and only substitute player as the team played in tank towns throughout the Midwest. After the team sported a 101-6 record, Saperstein instituted still another name change—the Harlem Globetrotters. Saperstein chose "Harlem" because it was to his black players as "Jerusalem is to us. And Globetrotters? Well, we had dreams. We hoped to travel." And travel they did, compiling a record of 296-26 playing "straight" basketball over the next two seasons.

But with the Depression bearing down on the country, and with potential opponents becoming more and more unwilling to lose money by asking customers to come see their hometown teams being trounced, Saperstein made a monumental decision. Starting in 1930 the Globetrotters undertook a fancy, comedic razzle-dazzle game plan that quickly made them a must-see attraction on the barnstorming circuit. Still, Saperstein was forced to pinch pennies— avoiding hotels by having the players sleep in the car while he drove to their next game, avoiding restaurants by buying loaves of bread and tubes of bologna—until 1940, when the Globetrotters first started showing a profit.

That same year the team won the World Basketball Championship, played in Chicago, and went on to win something called the International Cup in 1944. Then on February 19, 1948, the Trotters played it straight in defeating George Mikan and his Minneapolis Lakers teammates, who had recently become champions of the National

Basketball League (and were soon to join, and dominate, what came to be called the National Basketball Association).

Black newspapers headlined the victory, but the white media focused only on the game's attendance (MIKAN, TROTTERS THRILL 17,823) or on the individual scoring battle between Mikan and Goose Tatum, the Globetrotters' center (MIKAN COOKS TATUM'S GOOSE).

Of course, the Harlem Globetrotters became—and still are—an iconic organization that has played before kings, popes, heads of states, and millions of adoring fans all over the world. However, Saperstein's reputation as enhancing the cultural and financial status of black athletes is sadly mistaken.

Once the Globetrotters became an international success, Saperstein decreed that only two players on the team came from big cities like New York, Chicago, and Detroit. He considered such players to be potential troublemakers. Indeed, the most critical advice passed on from the veterans to any newcomers who gained their trust was "Don't make waves." The threat of being fired was always active, and any teammate could turn out to be an informer.

For years the players wanted to cancel dates in Orlando, Florida, because the games there were always played outdoors on a cement floor in the wintertime. But the hearty gate receipts earned there caused Saperstein to turn them down.

It's understandable that Saperstein had to limit his expenses until the Globies started making big-time money. Still, when the team became enormously profitable, the players averaged only about a hundred dollars per week during a normal four-month tour. If they had to play a doubleheader, they were given a bonus of twenty-five dollars.

Another way to save money was to issue each player a single uniform for the duration of a tour that they were responsible for cleaning. But the uniforms were thick, blanket weight, and because they needed several days to thoroughly dry, they were always moldy and smelly. Most of the players wore Band-Aids on their nipples to keep them from being rubbed raw. A few more measly dollars were saved by not supplying oranges for the players to suck on during halftime.

To uphold the glamorous Globetrotter tradition, the team stayed in the most fashionable hotels in whatever city they were playing. The hotels were so expensive and so isolated that a normal breakfast would consume most of a player's fifteen-dollar per diem meal money. Of course, Saperstein was happy to advance them moneys from their next check. "We were always in the hole to the company store," said one player.

The players called Saperstein "patronizing" and "colonial." Saperstein called the players "Oscars."

Celebrities such as Sugar Ray Robinson, Lou Brock, Ferguson Jenkins, Bob Gibson, and Bill Cosby made guest appearances. So did Muhammad Ali, who alienated the players by agreeing to help them with a proposed strike aimed at raising their wages—and then reneged.

Wilt Chamberlain also joined the team during the 1958-59 season while waiting for his freshman class at Kansas to graduate and thereby making him eligible to play in the NBA. One day the fans in attendance went crazy over Wilt's dunks and paid no attention to the antics of Meadowlark Lemon. Once the stands emptied Lemon challenged Chamberlain to a game of one-on-one. Teammates laughed, knowing that—despite his trick shots—Lemon was about as talented as an average high school player. In fact, they despised Lemon—an inferior ballplayer who was the center of every play in every game.

It was no surprise to anybody except Lemon when Wilt beat him 11-0 without raising a sweat. But once inside the locker room, Meadowlark attacked Chamberlain from behind with a Coke bottle. Wilt caught him in midair and lifted him high overhead as though Lemon were a barbell.

Lemon was advertised as "the Clown Prince of Basketball" and, unknown to his teammates, earned one hundred thousand dollars annually. After getting thoroughly humiliated by Chamberlain, Saperstein had to pacify Lemon by increasing his salary.

"Most of us," said one of Saperstein's players, "still had NBA aspirations and considered ourselves to be serious players. It was tough for us to ignore our natural talents and play like clowns. We had no sense of pride. We had to live in the past to find any satisfaction out of playing basketball."

A players' union was formed in 1971, five years after Saperstein died and his heirs sold the team. But during Saperstein's penny-pinching, semiracist regime, what was the allure of being a Globetrotter? "You get hooked on the travel, the adulation of the fans, the good life," said one player. "But mainly, you get hooked on the pussy. I mean, copping pussy is easier than scoring against the Generals."

Testimony: Charley Rosen

In the fall of 1991 I became the coach of the Oklahoma City Cavalry, an expansion team in the minor-league Continental Basketball Association (CBA).

OK City . . . The wildest West, where even the shortest drink of water proudly wore a ten-gallon hat. Where barbecued anything (including bologna) was treasured as being top-of-the-line eats. Where the airport was named after Wiley Post, who perished in an airplane crash.

I was officially welcomed to town by Abe Leamons, the legendary cornpone coach of Oklahoma City University, who said this: "So you're the Jew coach from New York that's gonna set this town on fire?"

That same week I filmed a TV commercial for the Cavalry. I wore a team jersey, team shorts, and sneakers. A long, bushy fake beard made of steel wool was taped to my face, and I also wore a small, round red cap—the bright color supposedly used to distinguish it from a yarmulke. It's a wonder that the makeup person didn't place another hump on my already oft-broken nose. I was to play a one-on-one game with a small, frail eighty-year-old woman who had been reporting on local weather for an OKC TV station for several decades. I was introduced by an off-camera narrator as coming from New York City, having "strange habits," and smelling of "strange New York foods."

As the "game" began I was clearly the villain, pushing and elbowing my opponent . . . until she "stole" ball and (with an unseen lift from me) dunked the ball for the winning score. The ad was shown repeatedly and, after the season, won a prestigious statewide award.

Also, during the season, several fans came up behind me to inspect my backside and to speculate in not-so-soft whispers that my pants must have been specially tailored to hide my tail.

8

....

About All-Americans, Blackbirds, the Olympic Games, and the Rosenblums

There had been no shortage of excellent Jewish basketball players from the beginnings of the sport through the 1930s. It was much easier to be officially designated as an outstanding player back then because so many organizations published their own versions of All-American teams. These included the Amateur Athletic Union, Associated Press, United Press International, *Sporting News*, Helms Athletic Association, *College Humor* magazine, Christy Walsh Syndicate, *Converse Yearbook*, *Literary Digest*, Newspaper Enterprises Association, Madison Square Garden, and just about every newspaper in the country.

Here, then, were the Jewish basketball players so honored:

Maclyn "Mac" Baker, Robert Lewis, Milton Schulman—NYU
Louis Farer, Bernard Fliegel, Moe Goldman, Pincus "Pinky"
    Match, Moe Spahn, Ira Streusand—CCNY
Louis Bender, William Laub, Samuel Melitzer—Columbia
Jules Bender, John Bromberg, Danny Kaplowitz, Ben "Red"
    Kramer, Irving Torgoff—LIU
Max Kinsbrunner, Nathan Lazar, Max Posnack—St. John's
Ed Wineapple—Providence
Louis Hayman—Syracuse
Jerry Nemer—Southern California

Herbert Bonn—Duquesne
William Fleishman—Western Reserve
Marvin Cohen—Loyola of Chicago
Meyer Bloom—Temple
Bernard Opper—Kentucky
Cyril Haas, Carl Loeb—Princeton
Leon Marcus—Syracuse
Sam Pite—Yale
Emanuel Goldblatt—Pennsylvania

In addition, not counting the above All-Americans, the following Jewish players were selected to All-Ivy League teams during that same period:

Solon Cohen, Peter Gitlitz, Ed Horwitz, Louis Nassau, Joseph Weiner—Yale
Leonard Hartman, William "Red" Laub, Jack Rothenfeld, Samuel Schoefeld, Samuel Strom—Columbia
Karl Friedman—Dartmouth
Louis Freed, Louis Hatkof, E. Schlossbach—Cornell
Henry Kozloff—Pennsylvania

Note how many of the above played for eastern colleges, the only reason being that the vast majority of the nation's Jews lived there.

Coached by Clair Bee, the Long Island University Blackbirds were easily the best collegiate team in the mid- and later 1930s. They had two undefeated seasons—1936 (26-0) and 1939 (25-0). In both of those seasons, the overwhelming majority of relevant sources considered the Blackbirds to be the national champions. Indeed, in April 1939, LIU secured this title by winning the second edition of the National Invitational Tournament (NIT). And it was no surprise that the rosters of both of those invincible squads were predominantly Jewish, as were virtually all of the starters.

On the 1936 team were Ben Kramer, Leo Merson, Jules Bender,

Archie Kameros, and Willie Schwartz. The 1939 outfit included Irving Torgoff, John Bromberg, Daniel Kaplowitz, Solomon "Butch" Schwartz, George "Dutch" Newman, Max Sharf, Solly Cohen, and Irv Schneider.

Another reason for LIU's successes was Bee's conducting four-hour practices six days a week, with only a three-hour session on Sundays. Moreover, since there was no gymnasium on the LIU campus, until they became national champs the Blackbirds played their home games at the nearby Brooklyn College of Pharmacy gym that seated only eight hundred. Bee tailored his game plan to fit the tiny court—inventing and employing a stifling 1-3-1 trapping-zone defense.

Faced with stiff competition from other metropolitan powerhouse programs—mainly CCNY, NYU, and St. John's—how was Bee able to recruit such outstanding local talent? Critics claimed that Bee took advantage of both LIU's lax academic standards and the absence of any oversight by the fledgling National Collegiate Athletic Association (NCAA). For example, for most of his career at LIU Jules Bender was a nonmatriculated night-school student and theoretically ineligible to play any varsity sport.

One of Bee's players remembers the money that was always available:

> My job was to shoot fifty foul shots a day. Once a week I'd go and pick up an envelope at the Bursar's Office. My average salary amounted to about eight dollars a week. Sometimes there'd be as much as fifteen dollars in the envelope if I had a good ball game. Then I found out that most of my teammates were making more than me, so I went to Bee and complained. I told him that my mother was working to support me. Right after that, the school started to send my mother twenty dollars a week.

In the early 1930s Bee also coached football and baseball at LIU. According to Archie Kameros, "The day before a football game, Bee would head for a coal mining town in Pennsylvania and recruit a team to represent LIU. Who knows how much money changed hands?"

Kameros reported that Bee's baseball teams also benefited from illegal recruiting:

> In 1933, he had a baseball player named Barnes who wasn't even enrolled at LIU. Then there was one day in 1935 when Bee desperately needed a pitcher for a game against Princeton. Ken Norton had a sore arm and Marius Russo had pitched the day before. Bee came up with a guy named Mike DiVito, who happened to be enrolled in NYU at the time. DiVito was at NYU on a baseball scholarship but was temporarily ineligible because of low grades. DiVito pitched and won the Princeton game for the Blackbirds. Later that same season, DiVito regained his eligibility for NYU and pitched for them in a game *against* LIU. Most of the New York coaches came from the same neighborhoods. Some of them had relatives who came over on the same boat. It was a closed fraternity and nobody would ever think of ratting.

The LIU Blackbirds were not the only collegiate powerhouse basketball programs to feature Jewish players in the 1930s. As evidenced in the previous list of Jewish All-Americans, Syracuse, Columbia, Southern California, NYU, Western Reserve, Temple, and Kentucky likewise featured outstanding Jews.

It was no accident that, since most of the country's Jews lived in and around New York City, the rosters of the most powerful metropolitan colleges were filled with Jewish players. So it was that, no doubt inspired by the incredible successes of the Wonder Five, St. John's continued recruiting Jewish players. In the 1930s the best of these were Reuben "Rip" Kaplinsky, who was captain of the 1938 team that went 18-4; Java Gotkin; and Ralph Dolgoff. In 1937 the best player for another Catholic University, Loyola of Chicago, was Marvin Colen, a second-team Converse All-American. Meanwhile, from 1932 to 1934 Nat Holman's CCNY Beavers compiled a 43-3 record with teams composed almost entirely of Jewish players who were born and raised in New York City.

NYU was still another program whose excellence depended on

its Jewish players. Captains of the Violets during this decade were George Newblatt, 1930 (13-3); Sid Gross, 1935 (18-1); Willie Rubenstein, 1936 (14-4); and Milt Schulman, 1937 (10-6). In addition, Rubenstein, Gross, and Irwin "King Kong" Klein led the 1934 Violets to an undefeated (16-0) season. Add two more Jews—Schulman and Len Maidman—to the mix, and that 1935 team was deemed to be the national champions.

The 1936 Olympic Games took place in Berlin and were hosted by Adolf Hitler. Immediately prior to, and throughout, the Games, the Nazis ceased their anti-Semitic propaganda and tried to present their capital city as a model Potemkin village. However, the head of the U.S. Olympic Committee was Avery Brundage, a notorious Jew hater, who successfully schemed to limit the number of Jews on the American teams—and also to prevent several Jews from winning gold medals. Indeed, one of Brundage's most infamous acts was to convince the coaching staff of the track team to leave Marty Glickman off the 400-meter relay team in the gold-medal race. But there was nothing Brundage could do to alter the composition of the U.S. basketball team.

Basketball had been a "demonstration sport" in the 1904 Olympic Games (the third such international convocation), held in St. Louis. Three American colleges—Hiram, Wheaten, and the University of Latter-day Saints (which eventually became Brigham Young University)—competed in a round-robin tournament. The Hiram squad was 2-0 and was awarded facsimile gold medals. The 1936 competition was an "official" one and included basketball teams from twenty-one nations.

The composition of the original Team USA was determined by a tournament held in April at Madison Square Garden. The participants included the two finalists of the previous AAU Championship competition (the McPherson Globe Refiners, from West Texas, and Universal Studios, from Hollywood), the winner of a national YMCA tournament, as well as six college squads. The undefeated

LIU Blackbirds routinely started four Jewish players and voted to refuse an invitation to the trials as a protest against the Nazis' institutionalized anti-Semitism.

In the final game of the trials, Universal Studios defeated McPherson, 44–43. Accordingly, the U.S. team was composed of seven of the winning team's players, six from the losing team, and one from the tournament's third-place finisher, the University of Washington. A key player on the team was five-foot-ten, 150-pound Sam Balter, a Detroit-born Jew who, during his collegiate career, had been the captain of the basketball team of the University of California at Los Angeles (UCLA).

When the U.S. squad arrived in Berlin, they were faced with two alarming rules that governed international competition: no player could be taller than six foot two, and only seven players were permitted to be in uniform for any team in any game. Because the American team included two six-foot-eight and one six-foot-seven players, the rules committee yielded to their protest on the height limitation. And the Americans adhered to the second prohibition by simply dividing their fourteen-man squad into two seven-player teams—the entire Universal Studios team was one outfit, and the six McPherson players plus Ralph Bishop from Washington made up the alternate team.

Breezing through the tournament, the U.S. squad faced Canada in the gold-medal game. All of the games had been played outdoors on a clay and sand court, but a heavy and continuous rain turned the playing surface for the final game into a muddy quagmire. The Canadian team was coached by a Jew, Julius Goldman, who, like Balter, was born in Detroit. Goldman preached a fast-breaking, up-tempo offense that was unfortunately stymied on the sloppy court. On August 16 it was McPherson's turn to play, and they won, 19–8. There were no seats for the nearly one thousand spectators, who were forced to stand at courtside throughout the game in a chilly, driving rain.

All members of the victorious USA team were awarded gold medals, but only the McPherson players had the honor of accepting their medals from the hands of James Naismith in a postgame ceremony.

Throughout the tournament Balter's ballhandling skills emerged as a key factor in the two games he played. And it's quite probable that both Hitler and Brundage were pleased that Balter did not participate in the medal-presenting ceremony.

In a totally unofficial competition, Bishop beat Balter in the finals of a table-tennis tournament that was open to all members of the entire U.S. contingent.

The Berlin Olympics constituted Balter's last hurrah as a player. A year later he began a new career as an all-purpose radio announcer. In 1939 Balter became the first-ever sports commentator whose voice was heard from coast to coast.

Max Rosenblum was born on December 5, 1877, and arrived in Cleveland with his family when he was six years old. From a lowly beginning as an errand boy for a local clothier, Rosenblum eventually owned and operated a highly profitable clothing store in Cleveland. In 1919 Rosenblum bankrolled a basketball team made up of former college stars, primarily as a way to gain cheap publicity. At first the team was called the Rosenblum Celtics, then the Cleveland Rosenblums, and finally the Cleveland Rosies. Taking on all comers, the initial squad team compiled a record of 18-2 and was hailed by Cleveland sportswriters as "the recognized champions of Ohio." Rosenblum's early teams featured only a few Jews, most notably Marty Friedman.

Then in April 1925 Rosenblum hosted an organizational meeting at the Hotel Statler in Cleveland with the aim of establishing a professional basketball league—initially called the National Basketball League but soon changed to the American Basketball League. Several rule changes were put into effect: cages were outlawed, all baskets must be attached to backboards, the two-handed dribble was forbidden, and to ensure stability players were signed by each team to exclusive written contracts that averaged about fifteen hundred dollars per month.

For its inaugural season the ABL had franchises in Cleveland; Washington DC; Brooklyn, Buffalo, and Rochester, New York; Fort

Wayne, Indiana; Boston; Chicago; and Detroit. And the *Pittsburgh Press* reported that Rosenblum was "the leading spirit" of this new venture.

With no Jewish players (and, in fact, no Jews ranked among the ABL's leading scorers), the Rosenblums nevertheless finished the regular season at 23-7 before besting the Brooklyn Arcadians in a three-game series for the championship. Attendance for the opening two games of the series averaged about ten thousand in Cleveland, providing plentiful advertising for Rosenblum's store and creating unbridled optimism for every team in the league. Perhaps, Rosenblum might have thought, there was more money to be made in men running around half-clothed than from dignified men dressed to the proverbial nines.

For the 1926–27 campaign the Buffalo Braves folded, as did the Brooklyn Arcadians. But new franchises were established in Baltimore and Philadelphia, and the Original Celtics replaced the Arcadians, playing as the Brooklyn Celtics. In the championship series it was the Celtics who prevailed over the Rosenblums.

The ABL played musical franchises for the next few seasons, with the Rosenblums winning titles in 1929 and 1930. At the end of that latter season, a Jewish player was finally cited among the leading point makers—Nat Holman, who averaged 4.8 points per game for a team that opened the season in New York, moved to Syracuse, and wound up in Chicago.

Then the ABL collapsed under pressure from the Great Depression, and in the aborted 1930–31 season Davey Banks was second in league scoring at 7.5 points per game. Sadly, Cleveland would not field another professional basketball team for sixteen years. Yet if pay-for-play hoops was kaput in Cleveland, the ABL would be resurrected in two years and prove to provide a showcase for numerous Jewish basketball players.

Testimony: Omri Casspi

In 1999 Israeli-born Oded Kattash was signed to a contract by the New York Knicks but failed to make the team. Ten years later the

Sacramento Kings drafted another Israeli, Omri Casspi, in the twenty-third round, and he subsequently became the first of his nation to play in the NBA.

Casspi's early NBA career was disappointing, and he became a fixture on the league's merry-go-round. The Kings traded him to Cleveland in 2011, but the Cavs were not interested in re-signing Casspi when his contract expired in 2013. That's when he joined the Houston Rockets as a free agent. However, his stay in Houston didn't last long. After a desultory season in which he averaged 6.9 points per game as a strictly marginal player, he was traded to the New Orleans Pelicans, who promptly cut him.

The near-unanimous evaluations of his game by NBA scouts, coaches, general managers, and players was that, while Casspi was quick, lively, and talented, he was too soft to be a meaningful player. At the time of Casspi's dismissal from New Orleans, I was a featured NBA opinionator for Foxsports.com, and, in one of my columns, I seconded the universal opinion of his fatal flaw.

In a move that surprised most NBA watchers, the Kings reached out to Casspi in 2014 and invited him to return to Sacramento. It was an opportunity Casspi couldn't refuse. Even more surprising were Casspi's evolved toughness and vastly improved play on his second go-round with the Kings.

Through it all Casspi posted numerous entries on his Facebook account, many of them in Hebrew. There was (and is) no question of his pride in his religion and his homeland.

Early in the 2015–16 season Casspi routinely came off the bench for Sacramento and performed admirably. Even so, the Kings were a dysfunctional outfit, and there was considerable (and public) antagonism between their new coach, George Karl, and their best player, DeMarcus Cousins. After winning only one of their first eight games, the intrasquad atmosphere became toxic. Then, in a dramatic fashion, a players-only meeting seemed to spark the team, and their games suddenly became highly competitive and highly successful.

Here's what my reaction was to the Kings' improvement in a piece

I wrote for Todaysfastbreak.com, another NBA website: "Forget about the much-heralded team meeting, as well as the good vibes resulting from George Karl's publicized patting of DeMarcus Cousins' back. There's one overwhelming reason why the Sacramento Kings have turned their season around—putting Omri Casspi into the starting lineup."

When I contacted Chris Cooper of the Kings' public relations department requesting a phone interview with Casspi for this book, the response was shocking. He started off by asking me (via e-mail) if I was a fan of Omri's—a silly and inappropriate question. Then, while saying that he had no objection to my writing whatever I wanted, Cooper more than implied that Casspi was unwilling to talk to me because of the "negative" things I had written in the past. And so Casspi didn't respond to my request.

So, despite all the wonderful things Casspi has done to try to bring about understanding in the Mideast, I couldn't help feeling that he still was not a total mensch.

9

....

The SPAHS, the Crown Jewels, and the ABL

Less than a year after the first incarnation of the American Basketball League folded, the Metropolitan Basketball League came into being. John J. O'Brien, who had been the last president of the ABL, also presided over the MBL. The new league's abbreviated season began on February 10, 1932, with the third (and final) playoff game played on April 25.

Two of the seven teams involved were situated in New Jersey (the Union City Reds and the Hoboken Lisas), and two played their home games in Queens (the Long Island Pros and the Jamaica St. Monicas). The remaining franchises were located in Brooklyn, including the Brooklyn Jewish Center and a survivor of the ABL, the Brooklyn Visitations. The third Brooklyn team featured four players from the St. John's Wonder Five—Rip Gerson, Matty Begovich, Mac Kinsbrunner, and Allie Schuckman. Davey Banks rounded out the Jewels' starting five. With Kinsbrunner (8.3) and Schuckman (8.0) emerging as the league's top two scorers, the Jewels and the Visitations both finished with 10-2 records. Led by another Jew, Willie Scrill, the MBL's third-leading scorer (6.9), the Visitations defeated the Jewels in a three-game playoff to claim the league's championship.

Eleven teams kicked off the second (and last) MBL season, but only four teams were left when the playoffs commenced on March

31, 1933. Eventually, the Jewels swept the Union City Reds in two lopsided games in the championship series. Immediately thereafter, the Reds ceased operations and the MBL was defunct.

The players from the four surviving MBL teams—the Brooklyn Jewels, Brooklyn Visitations, Bronx Americans, and Hoboken Thourots—cast about for another organization that would enable them to continue to play for pay. On October 21, 1933, these teams joined forces with two refugees from the Eastern League—the Philadelphia Hebrews (who changed their name to the Philadelphia SPAHS) and the Trenton Moose—to form the second incarnation of the American Basketball League.

This time the ABL had an even more distinctive Jewish influence. Fifty percent of the players were Jewish, as were the ten leading scorers—from Benny Borgmann (10.0) at the top to, in descending order, Moe Spahn, Nat Frankel, Cy Kasselman, Lou Spindell, Allie Schuckman, Mac Kinsbrunner, Shikey Gotthoffer, Louis Bender, and Paulie Adamo.

It was no surprise that the SPAHS and the Jewels were the league's most potent squads—or that the SPAHS won the championship. In fact, even as the league's stability was challenged by so many franchises folding, moving, and being bought and sold, Jews continued to monopolize the ABL for another decade: the SPAHS were league champions in 1936, 1937, 1938, 1941, 1943, and 1944. In 1938 the Jersey Reds were led by Moe Spahn and Moe Frankel in beating the New York (né Brooklyn Jewels) for the championship. And through it all Jewish players continued to dominate the annual leading-scorer lists.

Indeed, in the 1930s Jewish hoopers totally dominated the pay-for-play game. One of the SPAHS, Moe Goldman, was also an innovator. "I was the first center in those days," he said, "who could run and shoot. The rest of the centers were tall, gangly, and couldn't run. All I had to do was fake and go. I could shoot if they stayed back. I was the first center to be able to run and shoot, to dribble and pass, to do all those things. So I would say, without trying to be boastful, that I revolutionized the center position."

Despite the establishment of two rival operations, the National Basketball League (1937) and the Basketball Association of America (1946), the ABL survived in much-reduced circumstances until 1953. In the latter years ABL franchises became more and more localized— most were situated in upstate New York, New Jersey, and eastern Pennsylvania.

Even so, several Jewish ABL players went on to have either marginal or distinctive careers in the BAA/NBA: Petey Rosenberg, Irv Torgoff, Ossie Schectman, Sonny Hertzberg, Art Hillhouse, Leo Mogus, Ralph Kaplowitz, Fred Jacob, Nat Frankel, Mike Bloom, Moe Becker, Jack "Dutch" Garfinkel, and Leo Gottlieb. Other notable non-Jewish graduates of the ABL included Ray Felix, George Crowe (a future Major League Baseball star), Dick Holub, Buddy Jeannette, Matt Goukas, Angelo Musi, and Ed Sadowski.

If the ABL showcased numerous excellent Jewish hoopers, even the most marginal Jews rarely played in the National Basketball League. That's because franchises in the second coming of the ABL were clustered in the Northeast, a region that happens to contain the vast majority of Jews. On the other hand, throughout the course of its life span, the NBL extended into Wisconsin, Indiana, Iowa, Minnesota, Colorado, Virginia, Ohio, and Michigan, areas with minimal Jewish populations. Even so, a handful of Jewish players did manage to excel, including Irv Torgoff, recently graduated from LIU, the reigning NIT champs, and Nat Frankel, who had previously starred in the ABL.

However, perhaps the single most influential Jew who participated in the NBL was Nate Messinger, a referee. In March 1939 the Oshkosh All-Stars faced off against the Firestone Non-Skids in the best-of-five championship series. Messinger worked the first two games and, according to those sportswriters and disinterested spectators on hand, blatantly favored the All-Stars' burly center, Leroy "Lefty" Edwards.

James Schlemmer, a reporter for the *Akron (OH) Beacon Journal*, observed that the only reason Oshkosh won the second game to even the series was the bias of Messinger: "When Edwards was apparently driving his elbows deepest into the men guarding him, Messinger called the fouls on the latter, for preventing Edwards from going entirely through them, and when the Non-Skids as much as made contact with Edwards he called fouls on them for holding."

With Messinger on the floor for the fourth game, the All-Stars knotted the series with a 49–37 victory, in which Edwards scored twenty-five points. Once again it was clear that, because of Messinger's protecting Edwards, the All-Stars' center was allowed to play with "almost unhampered freedom." In the fifth and deciding game, Messinger was elsewhere, Edwards was limited to nine points, and Firestone captured the championship with a 37–30 win.

Still considered one of the NBL's top officials, Messinger—"who combines the best features of tobacco auctioneer, hog caller and cheerleader in his assessment of penalties"—worked several other regular-season and playoff games without any apparent bias. However, the questionable nature of Messinger's honesty would create a furor several years later during the initial championship series of the fledgling Basketball Association of America.

Testimony: David Blatt

On January 22, 2016, David Blatt was fired. This was despite the Cavs' record of 30-11, despite having a total regular-season record under his guidance of 83-40, and despite Cleveland's having taken the San Antonio Spurs to six games in the 2015 championship series without the services of Kevin Love and Kyrie Irving due to injuries.

LeBron James was quick to claim that he had nothing to do with Blatt's dismissal, a statement that's impossible to believe. If LeBron, as he says, didn't lobby the Cavs' front office to replace Blatt with assistant coach Tyronn Lue (one of LBJ's best buddies), then his surrogates certainly did. These probably include LeBron's agent, plus several of his teammates.

Blatt's firing prompted all sorts of reactions. His former peers were astonished. The Cavs players expressed surprise. Some media Muppets defended Blatt, while others proposed that he got only what he deserved. More to the point, however, were numerous virulent anti-Semitic responses on various social media sites. Blatt was called everything from a "Jew bastard" to a "Zionist prick." Suggestions were made that he "go back to Israel," "get a nose job," and simply "die."

If sports in America is the modern-day opium of the masses, then far too many people have overdosed.

10

....

The War Years

The war was raging in Europe, but, in the nearly two years before Pearl Harbor, there was time enough for three more Jews to be honored as All-Americans: Louis Possner from DePaul, another Catholic school; Oscar "Ossie" Schectman from LIU; and Moe Becker from Duquesne, still another Catholic university.

Once the United States joined the fray, while either waiting to be drafted or being classified 4-F because their height exceeded the six-foot-six maximum for military service, several more Jewish basketball players achieved or repeated All-American status: Schectman, Becker, William "Red" Holzman from CCNY, Harry Boycoff and Hyman Gotkin from St. John's, plus Jerry Fleishman from NYU. Even so, the competition among and within the various branches of the military was far superior to the decimated college game.

Like several of these players, Holzman enlisted soon after his college eligibility was exhausted. Instead of being drafted and ending up in the infantry, Holzman enlisted in the U.S. Navy during the summer of 1942. He said:

> I was stationed at Norfolk Naval base and placed in the morale unit, which drilled and exercised troops and maintained recreational facilities. In our time off we also played basketball against other

service and college teams. All of our games took place before enthusiastic, packed houses and the style of play was very physical. . . . Our coach, Gary Bodie, was an old chief warrant officer. He knew how to motivate. "Get your ass moving," he'd yell, "or you'll be on a ship to the Pacific tomorrow." We moved our asses. Our Norfolk team was real good. One year we won 31 of 33 games we played.

Indeed, in 1944, the Norfolk Naval Training Station team was voted the most outstanding squad in all the service branches. "Navy basketball," Holzman added, "helped me by giving me the experience of going against top athletes from all over the country, boosting my confidence, and convincing me that I could be a pro player."

Even though the ABL continued to function during the war, the rosters of every team in the league were thinned by the military draft and voluntary enlistments. But none of the team owners went to greater lengths than Eddie Gottlieb to rebuild their rosters while still remaining competitive.

Whereas the SPAHS had traditionally featured players from Philadelphia, Gottlieb began to recruit players from New York—most notably Jack "Dutch" Garfinkel and Irv Torgoff. Gottlieb went so far as to sign another New Yorker, Jerry Fleishman, who had enlisted in the U.S. Army and was stationed at Fort Jackson in Columbia, South Carolina. On weekends Gottlieb would arrange to fly Fleishman from Fort Jackson to wherever the SPAHS were playing.

One player that Gottlieb desperately wanted to add to his team was Joel "Shikey" Gotthoffer, perhaps the toughest player of the time. But Gottlieb was unable to fly him to and from games as he had done with Fleishman.

At the beginning of the 1942–43 ABL season, Gotthoffer was a nonmilitary supervisor at Wright Aeronautics in New York City, tasked with overseeing the building of engines for the B-21 bombers. On weekends he was able to join the SPAHS, but after playing in only six games, Gotthoffer was drafted and classified 1-A. Since his job at

Wright was deemed essential to the war effort, he entered the service as a private and was allowed to continue working there. However, once Gotthoffer was officially in the army, he was required to work double shifts until the end of the war. "I didn't play basketball," he said. "I had to sleep sometimes."

The SPAHS finished the first half of the 1942-43 season with a dismal 4-9 record but rallied to finish in second place behind the Trenton Tigers—who were led by Mike Bloom and Ace Goldberg—to qualify for the championship playoff series. Led by a miraculous seventy-foot basket by Torgoff to end the second quarter of the seventh and deciding game, the SPAHS were champs once more.

Over the course of the subsequent 1943-44 campaign, Gottlieb added two more outstanding Jews—Schectman and Herm Knupple— and faced off against the Wilmington Blue Bombers to defend his team's ABL title. "It was quite a rivalry between the SPAHS and Wilmington," Schectman recalled, "although I don't know what created it." Perhaps the friction between the teams was a result of some ancient animosity that existed between the two Jewish coaches— Eddie Gottlieb and Barney Sedran.

In any case Schectman did know exactly what happened during a game played between these two teams in Wilmington. "There was a skirmish on the court. The closest guys were wrestling with each other, and I stepped in to separate them. Some fan came out of the stands and punched me in the jaw." The blow landed on an impacted wisdom tooth, and Schectman had to be taken to a hospital.

The SPAHS took a 3-1 lead in the series, but the Bombers' relentless defense shut down their opponent's outside shooting and won the next two games. In the deciding contest Moe Frankel—a Jew that got away from Gottlieb—scored seventeen points, and Wilmington clobbered the SPAHS, winning 57-33 to secure the championship.

Wilmington and the SPAHS met again in the spring of 1945 in the first round of the postseason playoffs, with each team having added a valuable Jewish player—Art Hillhouse for Gottlieb's crew

and Ben Kramer for the Bombers. This time the SPAHS prevailed
and then went on to defeat Baltimore to win their fifth and last ABL
championship.

Red Auerbach has been rightly credited with forcing professional
basketball to accept the increasing presence of black players. During
Boston's dynasty (1957–69), Auerbach slowly increased the number of
blacks in the Celtics' starting lineup, the point where, in the 1964–65
season, Sam Jones, K. C. Jones, Tom Sanders, and Bill Russell were
on the court for the opening tip-offs.

Lost in the pre-NBA history of the game were the efforts of another
Jew to integrate the professional ranks. Sid Goldberg was the manager of the Toledo Jim White Chevrolets, an entry in the National
Basketball League in the early 1940s. Desperate to fill his roster with
so many players in the armed forces, Goldberg signed several blacks.
Knowing that the NBL was loath to lose whatever franchises they had,
Goldberg remembers, "I went to the league and told them, 'I don't
know what you fellows are going to do, but if you want me to stay
in I'm going to use blacks.' Some of them didn't relish it, I suppose,
because they thought it would bring problems. But I don't think any
of them objected."

And there were problems, especially in Oshkosh, Wisconsin. Goldberg said:

> I went into a hotel there to register the team, and they said, "We
> don't accept blacks." So I had no place for them to sleep. The blacks
> couldn't even go to a hamburger place. I had to go and get them
> hamburgers. The blacks had to sleep in the car. It was cold, and I
> remember taking the uniforms out and putting them in the car to
> use for blankets. I had a room, but I felt guilty so I went out and
> slept in the car with them. We were there for a two-game series,
> and the second night I finally found a place in Oshkosh. This guy
> had one room, and the blacks and I slept there.

The obvious point is that Jews were instrumental in trying to make a place for black players in the pro game and succeeded in doing so.

Testimony: Omri Casspi

I knew Chip Schaefer when he was the head trainer as Phil Jackson coached the Bulls and also when he was on the Lakers' training staff when Jackson was in Los Angeles. Chip was working for Sacramento when the Kings came to New York to play the Knicks, and we reconnected over dinner. He was agreeable to convincing Omri Casspi to talk to me after the next night's game.

When I approached Casspi in the visitors' locker room, he said, "A few years ago, you wrote something about me that was hurtful when I was down. You had a list of the softest players in the league, and I was on it." His black eyes flashed with a cold, well-nurtured anger. I mumbled some lame excuse that he didn't hear and that I don't remember, but I didn't mention that the "soft" label was told to me by several NBA insiders.

"I don't hold a grudge," Casspi continued, "and since you're Jewish and I'm Jewish, I will talk to you."

"Okay. Thanks."

Casspi is profoundly and perpetually aware of his being Jewish, and for him being Jewish does not mean being defined by the Holocaust. It means working on himself to be a better person. "More and more humble," he said. "More and more religious. It also means giving what I can to the poor, to my community."

Has he experienced any anti-Semitism in America?

"The fans in Sacramento have been great," he said with a shrug, "but there are several posters all over the city promoting the Kings and the players. And on several occasions, swastikas have been drawn across my face on those posters. That's an indication of the dangers Israelis face every day and almost everywhere. The truth is that Israelis are the toughest people in the world."

He's incensed by the bias of much of the American media: "When a terrorist attacks an Israeli with a knife and then is killed, the headlines in the newspapers say that a Jew killed an Arab. It's so hypocritical."

Nor does Casspi understand the reasoning behind this blatant bias: "Israel is the only democratic country in the region, and we're America's biggest ally there. But our future as an independent country is secure."

Even so, Casspi takes precautions when he's back in his homeland. "I avoid going to clubs, and I have to think hard about any appearances I might make in public places. This is something that all of us have to live with."

Casspi then noted that he would be escorting another group of NBA players to Israel the next summer. That's because, perhaps even more than being a professional athlete, Casspi sees himself as a goodwill ambassador for all Jews.

I next encountered Casspi when the Kings came to New York nearly a year later. This time he greeted me as though we were old friends. Then we exchanged candid opinions on the respective states of both the Kings and the NBA. So it turns out that Omri Casspi is indeed a mensch.

11

....

The Penguin and the Birth of the BAA

Despite the minimal successes and total failures of so many alphabetical professional basketball leagues, Max Kase, the Jewish sports editor of the *New York Journal-American*, was convinced that a pro league could still be profitable. Kase understood that for any such enterprise to succeed, franchises would have to be situated in large metropolitan cities such as New York, Boston, and Philadelphia.

Because of his position at the newspaper, Kase was acquainted with Walter A. Brown, who (among several other enterprises) was president of the Boston Garden. Brown was very interested and tried to convince Ned Irish, the president of Madison Square Garden, to come aboard, but Irish demurred. It was another Jew, Arthur Wirtz, who convinced Irish and in the spring of 1946 recruited several other businessmen to form what became the Basketball Association of America.

All of the original teams were owned or operated (or both) by successful entrepreneurs who owned professional hockey teams in the American Hockey League (AHL) or the National Hockey League (NHL) as well as the arenas in which these teams played. Besides the rather dim possibility of making money, their motivation for forming the BAA was to schedule events on those numerous dates when their arenas were otherwise empty.

Prospective franchises in Buffalo and Indianapolis eventually dropped out, leaving the prospective new league with two divisions and eleven teams. In the Eastern Division were the Boston Celtics, Washington Capitols, New York Knickerbockers, Philadelphia Warriors, Providence Steamrollers, and Toronto Huskies. In the Western Division were the Chicago Stags, Cleveland Rebels, Detroit Falcons, Pittsburgh Ironmen, and St. Louis Bombers.

While the BAA had the money, the teams, and the venues, they now needed a commissioner. A round, pudgy Jewish man who exaggerated when he claimed to be five feet tall, Maurice Podoloff was born in 1890, "in a little settlement about seventy-five miles from Kiev," he said. When he was three months old, his parents emigrated from Russia to "the golden land, where the streets were paved with gold." He recalled, "We lived for a year on the Lower East Side of New York and then for four years in Setauket, a suburb of Port Jefferson, where my brothers David and Jacob were born. My father worked in a shop making sneakers."

Abraham Podoloff soon tired of working for somebody else and longed to relocate somewhere where he would eventually be able to start his own business. He also harbored another driving ambition: that his sons would get the best education that their new homeland could offer. After learning about the glories of what was then known as the Yale Academy, the family relocated to New Haven, Connecticut.

They arrived in town via ferry, and Abraham left his family at the waterfront and immediately set out to find a business he could call his own. "The business he found," said his eldest son, "was selling kerosene, which was the source of all cooking and illumination at the time. The equipment he acquired included an antiquated horse, a covered wagon containing five gallon cans, and a residence on DeWitt Street."

Gradually, the business prospered to the point where Abraham sold it for a considerable profit. He then began a real estate company that shared a suite of offices with Samuel J. Nathanson, a lawyer. Another of Abraham's ambitions came to pass when Maurice was accepted into Yale in 1909. Six years later Maurice graduated from Yale Law

School and was immediately sworn in as a member of the Connecticut Bar Association, upon which he was accepted into Nathanson's law firm. "After some four or five years of practicing law," Podoloff said, "I joined my father in the real estate business, moving from one side of the office to the other. A. Podoloff and Sons, Real Estate and Insurance, was really quite successful. My father was semiretired; my brother Jacob took care of the insurance, and I did a land-office business in the care of twenty-two apartment buildings."

A key to the Podoloffs' success was the brothers' opportunity to act as "beards" for New Haven's Catholic Diocese. When the church wanted to buy property in and around town without attracting attention, the Podoloffs would undertake the transactions in their own names. The money thus enabled the Podoloffs to gain a controlling interest in the Industrial Bank of New Haven.

Eventually, upon the suicide of one Harry Walker—renowned as the "Ice King"—who couldn't compete with the advent of artificially made ice, the Podoloffs were able to purchase, and then complete, a partially erected building that was blueprinted to contain an ice rink as well as the capacity to store sixty-five tons of naturally cut ice. A significant inducement was that the Yale hockey team had already signed a contract obligating the team to pay twenty thousand dollars for a seven-year lease on the ice rink for its practice sessions and intercollegiate games.

With the elimination of the state's notorious blue laws that prohibited the staging of any and all sporting events on Sundays, the New Haven Arena soon became the residence of the New Haven Americans in the Canadian-American (C-A) League, which was a farm system of the NHL. To turn on the lights on other nights, a portable basketball court (which could be laid atop the ice in thirty-five minutes) was built to host college games.

Because Maurice was the oldest of the Podoloff brothers, he became the "governor" of the Americans. Al Sutphin owned and operated the highly successful Cleveland franchise in the C-A League and was particularly appreciative of Podoloff's business acumen. Podoloff was named secretary-treasurer of the C-A League in 1935, and a year later—almost entirely due to Sutphin's lobbying—he became the league's president. Concurrent with Podoloff's new responsibilities, the C-A underwent a name change and became the American Hockey League.

None of the businessmen involved were surprised when the AHL thrived under Podoloff's guidance. Even so, his round, squat physique and his rolling walk earned him a nickname that was never uttered in his presence—the Penguin.

Fast-forward to the spring of 1946. Before Arthur Wirtz gave his final approval to join the fledgling BAA, he queried Sutphin about whom the league's president might be. Sutphin revealed that he had offered the job to Asa Bushnell, who was once the czar of the Olympic Games (where he routinely proved himself to be a virulent anti-Semite) and was currently the overseer of the Eastern Collegiate Athletic Conference. But Bushnell's demand for a long-term contract at twenty-five thousand dollars per year made him unacceptable.

"What kind of job is Maurice Podoloff doing in the AHL?" Wirtz asked Sutphin.

"A good job" Sutphin responded.

"If Podoloff takes the job," Wirtz instantly responded, "then I'm all in."

The very next day Sutphin and Podoloff met in New York. "Even though I told Al that I knew absolutely nothing about basketball," Podoloff said, "they hired me for eight or nine thousand dollars—I forget exactly."

At the time, Podoloff had personally witnessed only one basketball game. "A Yale game," he said, "that's for certain, but I can't recall who the opponent was. I do remember, however, that Tony Lavelli was the star of the Yale team. He was a hook-shot artist, but I was more impressed by the fact that he was a virtuoso of the accordion. In fact, Lavelli later left professional basketball to concentrate on his musical career."

Nor did Podoloff ever issue any apologies about his ignorance of the game. "When I became the president of the BAA," he said, "everything I knew about basketball wouldn't have filled the bottom of a thimble. And when I retired from the job seventeen years later, I still didn't know anything about the game itself."

Why then was he hired? "I had complete integrity," he said, "and I also had a heart.".

With the titular head now in place, the organizational meeting was held on June 16, 1946, at the Hotel Commodore on East Forty-Second Street, adjacent to Grand Central Station. Some of the eleven representatives on hand wanted to identify Podoloff as the league's "commissioner," but he didn't like the idea. "It sounded too much like *commissar*," he said, "and was too suggestive of czarist Russia to suit me." Podoloff was also allowed to continue as president of the AHL.

Of the representatives gathered, Ned Irish had an excellent working knowledge of basketball promotion and advertising, as did Eddie Gottlieb, owner of the Philadelphia entry. But Gottlieb was the only participant who also had an *X*s-and-*O*s understanding of the game.

Their discussions covered everything from the distribution of gate receipts to the size of the numerals on the jerseys (ten inches in front, six inches in back), from the fine for forfeited games (five hundred dollars) to prohibiting the signing of any player whose freshman class had not graduated, and from defining Podoloff's powers to banning black players. But it was Gottlieb who proposed and explained the rules of the game.

Before he adjourned the meeting, Podoloff said, "Congratulations, gentlemen, you are now a regularly organized body."

Testimony: Oscar "Ossie" Schectman

The first game in BAA-cum-NBA history was played on November 1, 1946, with the home-standing Toronto Huskies downing the New York Knickerbockers, 68–66. And the first basket was scored by New York's sturdy point guard Oscar "Ossie" Schectman—a Jew.

When I spoke to him several years ago, the ninety-three-year-old Schectman had to turn up his hearing aid to participate in a telephone conversation, but not many of his recollections of that historic ball game had dimmed. "I scored on a two-handed underhand layup," he said, "which was the chippy shot back then. I also remember being on the receiving end of a give-and-go, but I can't remember who I received the pass from." Nobody paid much attention to Schectman's milestone until 1982, when Ricky Green of the Utah Jazz was officially credited with scoring the NBA's five-millionth point.

In 1996 the survivors of that initial game had a reunion as part of the NBA's fiftieth anniversary celebration. "That's when an old teammate of mine," said Schectman, "a guy named Nat Militzok, told me that he had made the pass, but I'm positive that Nat wasn't one of the starters."

Schectman was also certain about some other salient information: "I was the Knicks' third-leading scorer [8.1 ppg]. I also finished third in the league in assist average [2.0], and my salary was sixty dollars per game. Don't get me wrong, though. I have no jealousy or resentment over how much these guys make today. I think they're the best athletes in the world, and they're worth every red cent. I'm just proud to have been one of the NBA's pioneers."

What a nice man Schectman was: a joyful survivor from another generation; a creature from a world where the almighty dollar was not worshipped so devoutly and by so many; where athletes played basketball at the highest possible level, unconcerned about vying with one another for the biggest contract, the costliest bling, or the biggest posse; where sixty dollars a game was just fine; where somebody could do something (anything) just for the intrinsic joy of doing it. He recalled:

The ball was made of leather, and it was darker colored and much heavier than the one they play with nowadays. There was a rubber bladder inside that would have to be pumped full of air, usually at a gas station. And the outside of the ball was sealed tight with leather laces. The laces were slightly raised from the rest of the surface, so if you were dribbling and the ball landed on the laces, it wouldn't bounce up straight and you could easily lose control. By the beginning of the fourth quarter, the ball would become so lopsided that every pass, dribble, or shot was a perilous adventure.

Schectman's peers were the best hoopers on the planet, yet he could cite only a handful who would conceivably be able to compete with today's best. "Joe Fulks, for sure. Maybe Connie Simmons and Bud Palmer. We didn't have the size, the agility, or physicality. Players today have to be ambidextrous, and we never were. I was a point guard, one of the best ball handlers in the league, and I went left maybe once every game."

Dunking was out of the question. "Who could do such a thing? Maybe Fulks? George Mikan didn't come into the league until I was through, but I doubt if he could ever dunk. Besides, if you did dunk the ball, the refs would call you for basket interference."

Schectman noted other vast differences between the early days and now. "We all ran some form of a figure-eight offense that was predicated on movement, picks, and changes of direction. Stuff that came straight out of the settlement houses. Before Mikan most of the centers played the high post and were good shooters and passers. The best pivot man I ever played with was Dolly King, but back then no blacks were allowed in the BAA."

Although he didn't categorically criticize young whippersnappers, Schectman did reflect on some basic aspects of the game that the old-timers performed at a higher level than modern NBAers. "We moved better without the ball, and we played much smarter. Back then a good defender could stop a good scorer one-on-one, but that's not possible anymore. I think the way the women play in the WNBA is comparable to the way we played."

Even so, Schectman was a big fan of NBA action and watched the march of the seasons with a joyful heart. "We had thirty-foot range with our set shots," he said, "so I love the three-point line. I also like the recently instituted zone defenses, because it forces quick ball movement. And I think the NBA offenses are terrific. Why go through all the motions when they can get right to the shooting and the one-on-one situations? We needed all the cutting and running around to get open shots, but these guys don't. That's why the modern game is so much more exciting."

His hearing might have been be diminished, but the years had not darkened his luminous sense of wonder. "When I watch the games on the TV," he said, "I can't help projecting myself into the action. And it's a thrill to see guys like Steve Nash and Jason Kidd. Their fundamentals are outstanding—footwork, balance, shooting techniques, ballhandling skills. Contrary to what some of the old fogeys might say, I think their fundamentals are much better than ours ever were."

Schectman apologized for cutting short the conversation. "There a game on the TV that I don't want to miss," he says. "Phoenix versus Dallas, my two favorite teams. Believe me, the golden years are terrific as long as it's game time."

Before he could hang up, I sneaked in one last question: Any regrets?

"Sure," he said. "I wish I would have known how to do a crossover dribble. That really looks like a lot of fun."

Anything else?

"Not really. I always thought I wanted to be able to dribble between my legs, but that's something that started happening on its own about ten years ago."

12

·············

Too Many Jews on the Knicks

Since there was no mechanism to draft players in the BAA's inaugural season, teams had several choices to fill their rosters:

sign the best available collegiate players
outbid NBL teams for their best players
sign players who had proved their mettle in the various and
    highly competitive armed-forces competitions
in order to attract the largest number of fans and media publicity,
    sign college players who had excelled on local college teams
mix and match all of these options

The Knickerbockers chose to sign as many metropolitan-area hoops heroes as possible. Because LIU, CCNY, NYU, and St. John's were perennially among the nation's top college programs, it was anticipated that the Knickerbockers would have a powerhouse team. Also, since New York City still contained the largest population of Jews in the country, and since basketball was a secular religion to so many Jews there, it was no surprise when the Knicks' opening-day ten-man roster featured so many Jews. Indeed, according to Ned Irish, "good" players were those who would bring more fans through the turnstiles. He had no other criteria.

The Jews who started the season included Ossie Schectman, a

graduate of LIU who had played with the SPAHS in the ABL; Sonny Hertzberg, CCNY; Leo "Ace" Gottlieb, CCNY and another veteran of the ABL's SPAHS; Ralph Kaplowitz, NYU and the SPAHS; Nat Militzok, New York born who had transferred from CCNY to Hofstra and then to Cornell; Hank Rosenstein, CCNY; Stan Stutz, an import from Rhode Island State; and Jake Weber, an import from Purdue. The Gentile players were Tommy Byrnes from Seton Hall and Bob Cluggish from Kentucky.

Considering the makeup of the team, it was critical for the Knicks to hire an appropriate coach—which they certainly did not do. Irish desperately wanted to hire Joe Lapchick, a former Original Celtic and without question the most respected basketball strategist in the metropolitan area. But Lapchick was still contractually obliged to continue coaching at St. John's for another year. Since his first choice was not yet available, Irish turned to Neil Cohalan, one of Manhattan College's all-time best athletes and coaches, with the understanding that Cohalan would only be keeping the seat warm for Lapchick.

As an undergraduate Cohalan had earned varsity letters in basketball, baseball, football, and track and field. He became the Jaspers' basketball coach in 1929 and produced several outstanding teams (his total record was 165-80, with his best season being 18-3 in 1942–43). The war siphoned off many of the school's varsity athletes, and when the basketball program was shut down, Cohalan enlisted in the U.S. Navy in March 1944. After one year of sea duty, he was transferred to the Armed Guard Center, in Brooklyn, as an athletic officer. While there he coached the Armed Guard five to a record of 29-2, including the Third Naval District title. Cohalan was smooth and polished and was still hailed in the press as Manhattan College's "number one glamour boy." In some ways he had a little too much glamour, which manifested in an excessive fondness for alcohol.

Even so, Lapchick not only heartily endorsed Cohalan but also worked closely with the Knicks' coach, even to the point of taking an active part in the team's preseason training camp in the Catskills. Once the season was under way, Lapchick traveled with the Knicks whenever his scheduled permitted and also scouted rival ball clubs.

In any event, it was soon obvious that not only was the team old and slow, the big men unathletic to the point of being clumsy, but Cohalan was also in over his head. "Neil knew the college guys his Manhattan teams had played against," said Hertzberg, "but he wasn't at all familiar with either pro players or the pro game. He was used to teaching fundamentals to boys. And in college the procedure was to go with your five best players until somebody got hurt or fouled out. The pro game was more about balance and matchups and required more in-game management. Now you might need defense or rebounding. Now you might need scoring."

The schedule was likewise difficult for Cohalan to accommodate. "In college," said Hertzberg, "you might have one big game every week. In the BAA, we had three or four every week. Neil had trouble preparing us on a game-to-game basis, and being always on the go, moving from city to city, also wore him down in a hurry."

Still, since so many of the players were Jewish and from New York, they were a tight group. After home games they'd go over to somebody's apartment for beer and pizza or chicken while they rehashed the game. "We were so cohesive," said Hertzberg, "that it didn't make much difference who roomed with who on the road."

After a rousing 14-3 start, the Knicks plunged into a five-game losing streak, and by mid-January their record was 19-19. That's when Cohalan became utterly convinced that the many Jewish players on the team had become a serious issue. In Pittsburgh the fans greeted the Knicks' appearance on the court by singing their own version of a popular song: "East Side, West Side, here come the Jews from New York." In other cities, when the Knicks had the ball, the fans took to shouting, "Abe! Pass the ball to Abe!" These reactions prompted Cohalan to complain to Irish about the predominance of Jews on the team. Cohalan thought they were cliquish and invited too much fan abuse on the road.

An injury had already terminated Schectman's season, but Irish proceeded to trade Militzok to Toronto (for Bob Fitzgerald), Kaplowitz was dealt to Philadelphia (for Moe Murphy), and Rosenstein and Weber were sold to Providence. The midseason addition of Bud Palmer improved New York's final record to 33-27. They went on to defeat Cleveland in a three-game playoff series before being swept in two games by Philadelphia.

Meanwhile, Kaplowitz turned out to be the catalyst that boosted the Warriors to the BAA's championship.

There were several other Jews who distinguished themselves during that season:

Jerry Fleishman (4.5 ppg) was an important sub for Philadelphia.
Leo Mogus had 13.0 ppg with both Toronto and Cleveland.
Mickey Rottner, 7.6 ppg with Chicago.
Irv Torgoff averaged 8.4 points per game for the Washington Capitols.
The best Jewish player was Chicago's Max Zaslofsky (14.4 ppg), who later starred with the Knicks.

Journeymen Jewish players included Mel Hirsh, Moe Becker, Hank Lefkowitz, Irv Rothenberg, Lee Knorek, Nat Frankel, Petey Rosenberg, Red Mihalik, Fred Jacobs, and Ben Goldfaden.

During the postwar years several Jewish players were named to various college All-American teams. Harry Boycoff (1946) and Hyman Gotkin (1944 and 1945) continued St. John's tradition of recruiting stellar Jewish basketball players. Jack Goldsmith from LIU (1946) was a set-shot artist. Sidney Tanenbaum was an All-American guard for NYU in 1946 and 1947, with teammate Don Forman gaining the same honor in 1948. Still another NYU All-American in 1948 was Dolph Schayes, who would eventually develop into the best Jewish basketball player of all time.

Testimony: Dolph Schayes

Born in the Bronx on May 19, 1928, Dolph Schayes was one of the
NBA's first superstars. At six foot eight and 220 pounds, he was a ferocious rebounder and powerful driver, but he was also remembered as
being one of the last practitioners of the two-handed set shot. Indeed,
his trademark shot had such a high arc that it was called "Sputnik."

Schayes played his seventeen NBA seasons with the Syracuse
Nationals (1949–63), finishing his pro career in 1964 when the Nats
moved to Philadelphia. Among his accomplishments were leading
Syracuse to an NBA Championship in 1955, participating in twelve
All-Star Games, and being named to six All-NBA First Teams. His
most pertinent career statistics include averaging 18.5 points and 12.1
rebounds per game and netting 85 percent of his free throws.

If Schayes was sometimes criticized for lacking an inside post-up
game, his explanation brought up his Bronx roots: "My home court
was the Crescent Avenue schoolyard, where we mostly played three-
on-three, so moving into the pivot was frowned upon. We just played
the pure game of pass, cut, pick-and-roll, and spread the floor. It was
a game of motion, a game of movement. So we moved, and I moved,
and I learned the schoolyard game."

After leading DeWitt Clinton High School to a borough championship, Schayes was only sixteen years old when he enrolled in NYU
in 1948. "I never thought of myself as a Jewish basketball player,"
he said. "In the schoolyard, at Clinton, and with most of the high
school teams we played, just about all the players were Jewish. This
was also the case at NYU, when so many of the other local college
teams featured a host of Jewish players. I didn't really experience
any anti-Semitism until NYU went up against colleges from other
parts of the country."

For example, in the opening round of the 1948 National Invitational
Tournament, Schayes was NYU's young and naive freshman center
when he approached the center-jump circle to commence a game
against Texas. In a move designed to discombobulate Schayes, Texas

sent the five-foot-ten Slater Martin to contest the opening tip-off. Then, just before the referee tossed the ball into the air, Martin said to Schayes: "You Jew bastard."

"I've tried to forget that," Schayes said, "and I've almost succeeded."

While Schayes doesn't remember who won the ensuing jump ball, he does recall that NYU prevailed, 45–43. "We made it to the championship game," he said, "but Ed Macauley ate my lunch and St. Louis beat us by a bunch." The score was 65–52, with Macauley, a senior, outscoring Schayes 24–8.

Schayes recalls that the most "vicious" anti-Semitic epithets occurred when NYU played the Canisius College Griffins in Buffalo. "It got so bad, so loud, so intense, and so threatening that one of our players, Hank Ganzeppona, stood up on our bench and dared any of the fans to come over and say what they'd been shouting in the safety of the stands. Nobody took him up on it."

Once Schayes graduated into the NBA, only an occasional yahoo in St. Louis or Baltimore screamed some anti-Semitic epithets. "My entire focus was on playing the game," said Schayes, "so all of those cracks were just minimal background noise to me."

13

....

The Iron Man, Moe, and the Apprenticeship of Red Auerbach

Born in Homestead, Pennsylvania, on January 14, 1910, Paul Birch went on to become an outstanding basketball player at Duquesne University. Indeed, many contemporary observers believed Birch to be the best ever to play for the Dukes. After he graduated in 1933, he was invited to join, and barnstorm with, the Original Celtics, the highest possible honor at the time.

Birch quit the circuit in 1937 to coach a high school team in his hometown. "We won the state championship in 1938," he said, "then I went back to the Celtics for a year. In 1940, I started playing with the Fort Wayne Zollner Pistons in the old National Basketball League."

As Birch's playing career faded, he naturally moved back into coaching. "I wound up coaching the Youngstown Bears in the NBL," he said. "I actually liked working in a smaller city where my team was the only game in town."

Whether on the court or on the bench, Birch was always a ferocious competitor. While Birch was coaching the Bears, the smaller gyms enabled him to sometimes stick a foot onto the court and trip opposing players as they sped by. When he was caught, Birch would blame the tripped player for being too close to his bench.

His exploits at Duquesne were still legendary, so John Harris was eager to make Birch the coach of his new team in the BAA—the Pittsburgh Ironmen. "Pittsburgh was not a very appealing place for guys to play pro basketball," Birch said, "because baseball and football had a lock on the sports public. So I brought in some guys I had been coaching at Youngstown and added some locals who had played at Duquesne or at Pitt."

One of Birch's recruits was a Jew, Moe Becker—six foot one, 185 pounds—who had played at Duquesne and also under Birch at Youngstown. "I was supposed to sign with the Chicago Stags," said Becker, "until Birch took me out to dinner and convinced me to stay home and play for the Ironmen. Little did I know that Birch had changed his tune. Where he used to be easy to get along with in Youngstown, he turned into a monster in Pittsburgh. The two of us had trouble right from the start."

Press Maravich (Pete's father) was also signed by Birch and had this to say about Becker: "Perhaps it was Moe's good-natured view of the world that riled Birch. Moe's constant chatter kept all of us loose. Everything was a joke to Moe, and he was never serious enough about basketball to suit Birch."

Birch was always quick to praise Becker's shooting and offered this perspective: "We'd been on good terms in Youngstown, but for a variety of reasons, me and Moe didn't hit it off too well in Pittsburgh. Moe was a very sensitive guy."

Birch was unforgiving whenever one of his players made a turnover or took what he believed to be a bad shot. "Birch just kept yapping at us and never stopped," said Becker. "Every mistake we made was like a personal insult."

The first overt incident that ultimately led to the final showdown between Birch and Becker occurred when, early in a game in Philadelphia, Becker tossed up, and missed, a couple of long-distance two-handers before the Ironmen had a chance to set up their offense. Birch responded by blistering Becker with curses. "Actually," said Becker, "I settled down after those two shots and wound up playing a good game." Too bad Becker eventually fouled out and the Ironmen lost. That gave Birch an opportunity to rip Becker with even more virulent curses.

During halftime intermissions and also after losing games, Birch would routinely curse and throw chairs at offending players. Sometimes Birch would also throw a punch at his players. "We had to watch out for both his right and his left," said Maravich. "To protect ourselves, whenever he came close, we'd interlace our fingers and form a catcher's mask with our hands."

Nor was Birch averse to lashing out at opponents. "The Rebels had a player named Mel Riebe who was killing us in a game at Cleveland," Maravich recalled.

> Everybody was on edge and there were some fisticuffs between us and them—nothing really out of hand, just some harmless swings and a lot of bitching. But then Birch goes out onto the court and socks Riebe a good one, and suddenly the fans go nuts. Birch got scared and asked us to come help him out. No, sir. Not us. God almighty, we could've gotten killed with the crowd all angry like they were. So, we just hugged the sidelines until the cops came and calmed things down. Anyways, I guess Birch got a clue of what we all thought of him.

Since Becker had enjoyed a good relationship with Birch in Youngstown, he put his personal grievances aside for the sake of the team and went to his coach's hotel room after another disappointing road loss. "I told him how the team was falling apart," said Becker. "I also advised Birch to get close to the players—have a couple of postgame beers with us, anything to show that he was really a nice guy at heart. He wasn't very comfortable listening to what I had to say, but when we got back to Pittsburgh, he had a little shindig and treated us all to dinner. That helped some, until he went off again."

The discord that was brewing between Becker and Birch finally came to a violent boil on November 30, when the Ironmen were in Washington. The game was extremely physical, with a total of forty personal fouls being called. Here's Becker's version of what happened: "Irv Torgoff was with the Caps, and he was having a field day. Nobody could guard him, including me. Birch was always riding opposing players, and he called Torgoff a 'kike.' I resented this, and I cursed at Birch from my seat on the bench."

Birch kept after Torgoff, who tossed a few choice words at his tormentor. Their argument quickly escalated to the point where they swapped a few punches in the waning moments of the game. The refs instantly banished both of them. "Birch was already there when the players came into the dressing room," said Becker.

> I was so mad I was ready to attack him, but two teammates—John Mills and Hank Zeller—grabbed me, lifted me up, and put me in the shower to cool off. When I came out, another teammate, Stan Noszka, started to tell me that Birch didn't mean what he'd said to Torgoff as an anti-Semitic remark. By then, I was totally crazy. I thought Noszka was siding with Birch, so I squared off against him. The other guys pleaded with Birch to break us up and not let us start throwing punches. Birch just sat back and said, "Let the Jew take care of himself."

Red Auerbach was the coach of the Washington Capitols, and he later buttonholed Becker in the hallway. "I was so mad," said Becker, "that I was crying. Red told me that if Birch cut me, he'd find a spot on his roster for me." Two weeks later Becker was indeed put on waivers, but his rights were claimed by the team with the worst record in the league—the Boston Celtics—and he never got to play for Auerbach.

Here's Birch's rendition of the name-calling incident: "It was all a case of misunderstanding. All of the coaches were accomplished bench jockeys. To call a guy a kike or a Polack or a wop was common practice—anything to get under an opposing player's skin. Some of the other players came to Becker and asked why he was getting so upset. He was just a very sensitive guy. I was never prejudiced in my life. Hell, I used to play a lot of ball at the Pittsburgh YMHA."

Becker's NBA career consisted of that one 1946–47 season and a total of forty-three games with Pittsburgh, Boston, and Detroit.

Overall, he averaged 3.8 points per game. He remained in Pittsburgh, coaching at Braddock High School for many years. Becker died in Pittsburgh a few months after his seventy-second birthday.

The Ironmen finished the season with a record of 15-45, and Birch didn't make his NBA comeback until 1951, when his old boss Fred Zollner hired him to coach the Fort Wayne Zollner Pistons. Over the next three seasons, Birch's record was 105-102, plus 4-10 in playoff competition. Birch was fired after the 1953–54 season when he was publicly but unfairly implicated in a point-shaving scandal that plagued the Pistons and many other NBA teams.

Deprived of working in the game he loved, Birch descended into alcoholism, physical abuse toward his family, and poverty. He was eighty-one years old and living in a dilapidated shack in Pittsburgh when he died.

Arnold "Red" Auerbach was one of the NBA's most successful coaches and certainly among the most influential individuals in the history of the game. Yet many years before he led the Boston Celtics to their nine-championship dynasty, Auerbach had an ultimately disappointing apprenticeship as a rookie coach in the BAA's opening season.

Arnold Jacob Auerbach was Brooklyn born (September 20, 1917) and Brooklyn bred. As such he dabbled in all of the usual neighborhood sporting activities—stickball, punchball, Johnny on the pony, kick the can, box ball, off the bench (or stoop or curb)—but his first love was basketball. "I learned my basketball on a gym built outdoors," he said in a 1983 interview, "on the roof of Public School 122. Unless it snowed or rained, we played. In high school, I made the all-Brooklyn second team." Later whenever he was kidded about that second-class status, Auerbach's response was, "What people don't know is that we had more good basketball players in Brooklyn in those days than there were in the rest of the United States." What Auerbach failed to say was that virtually all of those Brooklyn players were Jewish.

The next stop for Auerbach was George Washington University (GW) in the nation's capital. "I had a tough time making the basketball team there," he said. "There were six backcourt men trying out for the varsity and only one spot open. I had four fistfights in the first two weeks of practice, but I got the job. The point is, I guess, I was always a bit brash."

After graduating Auerbach was good enough to play in the ABL, for the Washington Huerich Brewers. Over the next few years he also coached various local high school teams—starting with St. Alban's Prep School and finishing at Roosevelt High. Once the war erupted he landed in the navy and became assistant coach of the crackerjack Norfolk Naval Training Station quintet of 1943–44. "We had Fred Scolari and Bob Feerick and were one of the best teams in the country," he said. "On weekends, we'd do some local barnstorming for fifty bucks a game, and sometimes I'd play with them."

When Auerbach mustered out of the service in early 1946, he went back to coaching the kids at Roosevelt High while completing his master's degree at GW. "At the same time," he said, "I coached a team make up of some pro football players from the Washington Redskins, guys who were looking to make a few extra bucks in their off-season. A couple of times, we played in an arena owned by Mike Uline and that's when I first met him."

Auerbach's penchant for self-promotion served him well when he set his sights on advancing his coaching career: "I was twenty-nine and right out of the navy when I just walked in on Uline and told him I was the guy to coach his Washington team that was being organized for the new league. I was really a little nothing high school coach."

Auerbach's primary credential was the time he'd spent coaching in the navy, which led to his promising Uline that he would be able to assemble an outstanding ball club by recruiting the best players he had either coached or coached against. Uline, who didn't know a pick-and-roll from a kaiser roll, was impressed. "He offered me a one-year contract for five grand, saying that he'd had bad experiences signing some of his hockey coaches to longer-term deals. My school job paid twenty-nine hundred and I also had to teach hygiene and physical education, so I jumped at his offer."

Auerbach's biggest problem was that several of the players he successfully recruited were about the same age as he was. "I used to play with some of them," he said, "and all of us who had been in the service were certainly peers. But to maintain my authority, I had to keep my distance. So, sometimes I'd go to a movie with them when we were on the road, but that was the extent of my socializing. I made sure to stay away from their parties and their apartments. I knew I couldn't be picking some guy's kid up on my knee and then cut the guy two days later."

Auerbach also sought to emphasize that he was indeed the boss: "Some guys would start an argument every time I took them out of a game. So, I'd take those guys aside and say, 'Your job is to play, and my job is to coach. If I'm going to fail, it'll be because I can't coach and not because of your attitude. I'm not going to blow this job because I'm scared of you or anyone else. That's the way it is. Take it or leave it."

During the course of the regular season, Auerbach didn't come close to failing. He preached a fast-break game plan, and the Caps simply ran away from the majority of their opponents—finishing the regular season at 49-11.

But most of his players had a dim view of Auerbach. "Sometimes Red was charming," said Fred Scolari, "and sometimes he pissed us off. He would ask us to beat teams for different reasons. Maybe he didn't like the other coach. Or the other coach had told the press that we were vastly overrated. He had all kinds of ways to psych us up for games. This was new to me and to most of the other guys. We always played to win because that was what the game was all about. We didn't need any artificial reasons. Some of the older guys, like Feerick and Bones [McKinney], just ignored him."

Auerbach routinely stomped, shouted, spit at, and cursed the refs whenever a call went against the Caps. His antics created bad feelings among opposing players. "Red was always a clown," said Kenny Sailors, the mainstay of the Cleveland Rebels. "He'd do anything to get attention. All the other coaches hated him, because he thought he was such a genius, but it was Bones McKinney who actually ran the team. Bones kept the other guys in line, told Red when and who to substitute, and told Red what ought to be done to beat the other teams. We all thought that Red was little more than a figurehead—and an obnoxious one at that."

The BAA playoffs were a complicated situation. Because of the Capitols' outstanding record, they had to beat only the Chicago Stags to advance to the championship series. But the Stags stunned the Caps and closed out Washington's season in six games. Auerbach's players claimed that a major reason for their defeat was that the starters had played too many minutes during the season. "We were fatigued," said center Johnny Norlander, "and that was because Red never developed his bench players."

Auerbach coached the Caps to records of 28-20 in 1947-48 (failing to qualify for the playoffs by losing a tie-breaker game to Chicago) and 32-22 in 1948-49 (losing to the Minneapolis Lakers in the championship series). After the 1948-49 season Auerbach quit when Uline refused to give him a multiyear contract and was replaced by Feerick. The Caps franchise folded on January 9, 1951, in the middle of the season.

After a brief stint as an assistant coach at Duke University, Auerbach returned to the BAA (now called the NBA) to coach the Tri-Cities Blackhawks (28-29) in 1949-50. The following year he began his Hall of Fame career in Boston.

Testimony: Jordan Farmar

Jordan Farmar is a six-foot-two, 180-pound point guard who has had a varied career. Born on November 30, 1986, in Los Angeles, Farmar achieved All-American honors in high school and then at UCLA.

His professional career began with the Lakers, where he provided speed and quickness off the bench during the 2009 and 2010 championship seasons. Yearning to be a starter, however, Farmar signed a lucrative two-year contract with the New Jersey Nets. Then came stints in Israel, Turkey, back with the Lakers, with the LA Clippers, back to Turkey, and a return engagement in Israel. After completing the 2015-16 season with Maccabi Tel Aviv, Farmar joined the

Memphis Grizzlies on March 21, 1916. Over the course of the 2015–16 NBA season, Farmar and Omri Casspi were the only Jewish players in the league.

Farmar's family situation is just as varied. "My mother is a Christian," he says, "and my father is a black man, Damon Farmar, who played Minor League Baseball for many years. My parents divorced when I was two years old, and when I was four my mother married Yehuda Kolani from Tel Aviv. So, in my early years, I went from being raised as a Christian to being raised as a Jew."

Farmar has totally accepted Judaism as his religion. "It's part of my heritage," he says. "It's who I am. But I don't observe the Jewish holidays. I guess I'm more of a cultural Jew."

As part of his Jewish identity, Farmar has engaged in several philanthropic enterprises to promote relevant causes. In August 2008 he led a basketball camp for Israeli and Palestinian children, having them play together on the same team. A month later he joined the Chabad Telethon, shooting free throws to raise funds for a 250-year-old international organization dedicated to the welfare of Jewish people. Rabbi Chaim Cunin, executive producer of the telethon and chief executive officer (CEO) of Chabad of California, said, "Jordan is a real mensch. He raised $66,600 by making thirty-seven free throws in ninety seconds."

Yet Jordan's charitable endeavors are not limited to Jewish themes. For example, in the summer of 2009 he hosted the Jordan Farmar Celebrity Golf Classic, which raised funds to assist high-risk youths in the Los Angeles area as well as cancer patients at the Mattel Children's Hospital UCLA.

Farmar has a foot in two worlds, both of which have been subjected to various degrees of prejudice that's at best subtle and at worst deadly. But instead of seeing his Jewish-black background as a double whammy, Farmar takes the most positive aspects that these two cultures have to offer him. "I definitely inherited my athleticism from my father," Farmar notes. "But all three of my parents have been very understanding, letting me explore my blackness and my Jewishness.

My dad was at my bar mitzvah, and I'm very much connected to the black community. I'm kind of a chameleon."

His light skin caused some misunderstandings when he was younger. "When I used to play in the parks in black neighborhoods," Farmar recalls, "the guys who were talking about the matchups would always say, 'I got the white boy.' So I'd tell them that I was one of them."

Farmar's complexion also substituted an occasional anti-Semitic slur for any racial epithets from the fans who watched him play. He also contrasts his peaceful experiences in Turkey with David Blatt's constant feeling of being endangered when he coached there. "For sure it was strange when my teammates prayed to Allah to help us win a game," he says. "But I played well over there, and they supported me because my team was very successful and I was the go-to scorer. The basketball fans in Turkey do not like losing, and I think they had some antagonism toward Blatt mainly because his teams didn't win."

Through all of his travels, his ups and downs, Farmar is grateful for the warm reception he's received in Memphis: "An old black lady came up to me on the street the other day, gave me a hug, and said 'Shalom.'"

Farmar will be a free agent in the summer of 2016, but for now he's happy to be in Memphis, delighted to be back in the NBA, and happy with who he is. "The only thing on my mind," he says, as his latest team concludes the regular season, "is looking forward to helping the Grizzlies do well in the upcoming playoffs."

Unfortunately, Farmer was cut by Memphis prior to the 2016–17 season. He was then signed by Sacramento and cut by them before the 2016–17 season began, re-signed nine days later, and then cut again five days later. He is rumored to be playing back in Israel.

Rabbi Chaim Cunin was right: both on and off the court, Jordan Farmar is a bona fide mensch.

14

....

Gotty Wins Again and a Crooked Ref

If Philadelphia was justifiably celebrated as being a hotbed of professional basketball, then Eddie Gottlieb had set the fire. The popularity of Gottlieb's SPAHS convinced Pete Tyrell (who ran the Philadelphia Arena and the ABL's Philadelphia Rockets) that the new BAA team would be boffo at the box office. Since it wouldn't do for the SPAHS' nickname to be resurrected, the new franchise was named the Warriors, after Philadelphia's entry in the ABL (1926–28). In the same vein Tyrell had no qualms about putting the entire operation into Gottlieb's capable hands.

Gottlieb was proud and even thankful that he was a bachelor, since this status allowed him to work twelve hours a day. "He was married to basketball," said Harvey Pollack, who started as the Warriors' stat man before becoming their longtime public relations man. "Gotty did the Warriors' recruiting, negotiated the contracts, took care of all the traveling arrangements, booked the hotels, schmoozed the sportswriters and the local politicians, and, in his spare time, coached the team."

Most of the players signed by Gottlieb had three background experiences in common: several were local to the Philadelphia area and were graduates of either Temple or St. Joseph's, virtually all had played service ball, and the majority were veterans of the ABL. Still, his most important signing was born in a farmhouse on the banks of the small Tennessee River community of Birmingham, Kentucky. This was Joe Fulks, a six-foot-five, 190-pound forward who eventually became the BAA's first superstar.

Fulks was recommended to Gottlieb by Petey Rosenberg, a SPAHS alumnus, a St. Joe's grad, and one of the original Warriors. Rosenberg recalled:

> Nobody'd ever heard of Fulks when he played at Murray State Teachers College, but I'd played against him in a service tournament in Hawaii. Fulks was a sub on his team, but when he played he popped the ball into the basket like it had eyes. He could dribble, run fairly well, hit hooks with either hand, and he had a one-handed jump shot that couldn't be defensed. If Fulks couldn't play a lick of defense, well, back in those days, the only guys who did came from the Eastern Seaboard. Anyway, as soon as I could, I wrote a letter to Gotty telling him about Fulks. "If you sign this kid," I wrote, "you could win a championship in any league you could imagine." Fortunately, Gotty took my advice to heart.

Fulks would leading the BAA in scoring with 23.2 points per game, a whopping 6.4 more points than Bob Feerick, the league's second-best scorer. It was Fulks's sensational point making that forced Gottlieb to change his habitual game plan. Whereas his SPAHS outfits had been known for playing team-oriented ball with an emphasis on passing and cutting and a minimum of dribbling, the Warriors' offense centered almost exclusively on getting the ball to Fulks.

To pad Fulks's points, Gottlieb kept him on the court even if the Warriors were winning or losing by twenty points or more. "It was all about supply and demand," Gottlieb said. "As long as the fans want to see spectacular shots and a steady stream of points, we're going to try to please them."

Ever the promoter, Gottlieb was quick to capitalize on Fulks's high-volume scoring. The Warriors announced that fans could submit guesses as to how many points Fulks would have at the conclusion of the season. The guesses were to be jotted down "on a penny postcard" and mailed to the team's publicity department within a week. The winner would receive twenty tickets to a postseason playoff game. The response was numbered in the hundreds of thousands.

Except for instructing his team to feed the ball to Fulks, Gottlieb felt that pay-for-play players already knew the game and didn't require much additional instruction. He never put an X or an O on a blackboard and just let his players play. What Gottlieb did contribute to his team was intensity. He savored victory above all other considerations, while he suffered after each defeat as though another world war had been declared. "After a loss," said Petey Rosenberg, "Gotty would curse and rant and rave. And he'd keep on talking about the game, griping about all the things we'd done wrong from the start to the finish. I mean, he'd replay the game countless times on the train or on the plane. He'd just go over and over the goddamn game, dissecting every play again and again. After a loss, we tried to stay out of his way."

They could try, but Gottlieb would always find a way to corral his team and berate them just one more time. For instance, Angelo Musi described what occurred after the Warriors had lost an overtime game in Detroit: "We were in the airport, and our flight was leaving in thirty minutes, but Gotty just had to have a team meeting. The only private space at hand was a men's room, so he herded us in there and locked the door. He even stood leaning against the door to make sure we couldn't escape."

Gottlieb was furiously berating his players when suddenly there was a desperate knock on the door. Gottlieb cracked the door open, peeked outside, and saw a man with a strained look on his face. "What the hell do you want?" Gottlieb barked.

"I got to take a leak."

Without saying a word Gottlieb slammed and relocked the door and then resumed his tirade.

A game in Toronto was another example of Gottlieb's unquench-able quest for perfection. The Warriors were leading by twenty-six points with less than a minute left to play when one of them threw an errant pass. Gottlieb jumped to his feet and roared for his team to call a time-out. He was apoplectic as the players approached the bench. "What the hell was that?" he wanted to know.

"Cool down, Gotty," one of his players said. "We're a mile ahead, aren't we?"

"Does that mean you're allowed to get careless?" Gottlieb snapped. "Do something like that again and you'll all walk home."

After a so-so start, the trade for Ralph Kaplowitz energized the Warriors. Moreover, if Kaplowitz was able to feed Fulks enough to satisfy Gottlieb, he was also able to lay clever passes on Howie Dallmar and Angelo Musi. While Fulks continued to fill the basket, Kaplowitz's play made the Warriors' attack somewhat more diverse.

Philadelphia concluded the regular season at 35-25, fourteen games behind the Eastern Division–leading Washington Capitols, and Fulks totaled 1,389 points.

To open their postseason play the Warriors squared off against the St. Louis Bombers. Two days prior to the series (and the day after the regular season ended), Gottlieb took his entire team for a gala day of beach, sun, and beer at Atlantic City. "We were all impressed that Gotty wanted to win so badly that he covered all of our expenses," said Musi. "It was a great move on his part, one that really brought us all together." As a further incentive, Gottlieb vowed to chug five martinis if Philadelphia prevailed over St. Louis.

Even though the tenacious defense of the Bombers' Bob Doll managed to contain Fulks for the first two games, "Jumping Joe" exploded for twenty-four points as the Warriors won the deciding third game in St. Louis. On the flight back to Philadelphia, the teetotaling Gottlieb kept his promise and chugged five consecutive martinis. However, the players were sorely disappointed when the drinks had no discernible effect.

The Warriors then blasted the Knickerbockers in two lopsided games to earn a spot in the BAA's initial championship series. They were relieved when their opponents were the Chicago Stags rather than Red Auerbach's dominant Washington Capitols.

It was widely rumored—and ultimately confirmed—that one of the main reasons the Stags had upset the Capitols was the bias of Nate Messinger, a Jewish referee who worked all six of the games in the Chicago-Washington series.

Testimony: Eric Konigsberg

Back in the 2000–2001 season Charlie Ward and Allan Houston constituted the starting backcourt for the New York Knicks. Shortly after the season ended the two players were quoted in an article that appeared in the *New York Times Magazine*. The author of the piece was Eric Konigsberg, who had spent much of the season traveling with the team.

On several occasions Konigsberg tried to solidify his connection with Ward and Houston by attending Bible studies that the two players (along with teammate Kurt Thomas) regularly conducted in hotel rooms during road trips. Konigsberg, a Jew, revealed that the players were interested in his own religious practices and were particularly curious about Jewish dietary laws.

At one point Ward said to Konigsberg, "Jews are stubborn. But tell me, why did they persecute Jesus unless he knew something they didn't want to accept? They had his blood on their hands."

Houston, using his Palm Pilot, then recited a passage in the New Testament: "Matthew 26, verse 67. Then they spit in Jesus' face and hit him with their fists."

Ward then told Konigsberg, "There are Christians being persecuted by Jews every day. There's been books written about this—people who are raised Jewish and find Christ, and then their parents stop talking to them."

Konigsberg's article included everything Ward and Houston had said about Jews. The Anti-Defamation League was appalled and contacted the Knicks and the NBA to express their concern.

Here's how Ward responded to the ADL's distress: "I didn't mean to offend one group because that's not what I'm about. I have friends that are Jewish. Actually, my best friend is a Jewish guy, and his name is Jesus Christ. So therefore I have no reason to offend any religion or person of a religion because my best friend is Jewish."

But Ward wasn't done, yet his attempt to further explain his point of view got lost in his own tangled context. "My job as a Christian," he added, "is to let people know what Jesus did and how he lived his life. The context of the article is taken out as if Jews persecuted Christians, which biblically is what happened during that time. But if people want to be offended by what happened biblically, that's on them."

The ADL was far from mollified with Ward's answer:

We were shocked to read the comments of Charlie Ward and Allan Houston blaming the death of Jesus on Jews and accusing Jews of persecuting Christians. We had thought these destructive historic myths, which have been a source of anti-Semitism for centuries, were a thing of the past. However, we see that there are many good people who still hold these beliefs. In this attempt to clarify his comments, it is clear that Mr. Ward just doesn't get it. Sadly, he doesn't understand the impact of his comments and that they constitute anti-Semitism and religious bigotry.

15

....

The Fix and Close Shaves

In the early 1940s a high school mathematics teacher named Charles K. McNeal invented the point spread, thereby greatly facilitating betting on football and basketball games. The idea was to spot the weaker team in any given game several imaginary points, which made it possible and attractive for players to "fix" games in league with gamblers. So if Team A spots Team B five points but only wins by four, than whoever bet on Team B collects their payoff. It was possible, then, for players on Team A to win the game but deliberately "shave" the final margin to ensure that their team failed to "cover" the spread.

The temptation for players to be in league with gamblers was irresistible. Indeed, immediately after McNeal's invention, persistent rumors arose insisting that college players were already doing business. According to an LIU player:

Coach Clair Bee was in the merchant marines during the war, and Red Wolfe took over the team. Wolfe used to play for the SPAHS, and was very friendly with a bookie in the Bronx named Mike Manfield. Anyway, one night Mansfield informed Wolfe that several LIU players were shaving points, and even "dumping," that is, purposely losing otherwise winnable games. Wolfe then gathered us one day after practice and said, "I've played ball with most of your fathers, and I've known most of you since you were born, but if you dump I'm turning you in." We dumped the next game anyway and Wolfe kept his mouth shut. What else could he have done? Have the children of some of his best friends arrested? All he had to do was blow the whistle and Wolfe also would have become suspect.

The situation was no secret to anybody on the collegiate athletic scene. In 1944 Forrest "Phog" Allen, the highly respected coach at the University of Kansas, warned of a coming scandal that would "stink to high heaven." But gate receipts for college games were astronomical, and jubilant alumni were funding basketball scholarships by the dozens. A coach's organization was moved to reprimand Allen for showing "a deplorable lack of faith in American youth and a meager confidence in the integrity of coaches."

Then early in 1945 the New York district attorney's (DA) office was tapping the telephone of one Henry Rosen, whom they suspected of trafficking in stolen goods. Quite by accident they discovered that the supposed fence was also involved in fixing college basketball games. Surveillance was stepped up, and the full plot was quickly uncovered: five members of the Brooklyn College basketball team (four of them Jews) were implicated along with Rosen and another Jewish bookie, Harvey Stemmer.

Each player had already been paid one thousand dollars and promised another two thousand if he laid down in an upcoming game against Akron. It was also learned that one of the players was not even a registered student at Brooklyn. The gamblers were arrested, the ball game was canceled, and the other four players were expelled from the school in disgrace. "This involved only a local crowd," the DA said. One of the banished players disagreed, saying, "Every college team in the city is fixing games."

The city's lawmakers then amended a bribery statute to include gamblers who made bribe offers to amateur sportsmen. Betting rumors persisted, but the college game continued to thrive. Indeed,

Ned Irish extended his promotion of college games into arenas in Philadelphia and Buffalo. Irish could now offer a touring college team at least a lucrative three-day package. Basketball teams could play their way across the country and back without ever seeing a college campus. And if their schools were raking in the money, why shouldn't the players get their share?

Moreover, there was another forerunner of "the coming scandal" at CCNY. Paul Schmones was the star of the 1945 team. One of his teammates, Lenny Hassman, was a veteran dumper who realized that Schmones's cooperation was essential if business as usual was to continue. Hassman came to Schmones with an invitation to join in the fun. But Schmones took the offer straight to Coach Nat Holman, who kept the news a secret. Holman's reason was to avoid jeopardizing the large sums of money his team's games were generating. So Holman simply cited Hassman's weak grades and impending academic probation and dropped him from the squad.

Under Holman the trademarks of a CCNY basketball team were discipline, courage, persistence, and unquestioning obedience to their celebrated coach. When Holman blew his whistle during a scrimmage, the terrified players would freeze while they waited for his wrath to descend on whoever was out of synch. Holman pushed his players to (and often beyond) their limits. He taught them, he bullied them, but he let them share his dream. Together they would seek the perfect play, the faultless ball game.

In any case, there was a history of point shaving and outright dumping at several New York City colleges. Several local players even decided to attend CCNY, LIU, or NYU strictly because of the moneymaking opportunities that playing at these schools afforded.

However, except for the public blip at Brooklyn College and the secret problem at CCNY, the general public believed that the college game was straight and the players pure and honest. The pros, on the other hand, were considered to be little better than well-paid prostitutes. It was hard to find an honest game at any level of competition.

While known only to the close-knit BAA community, Nate Messinger's crooked work greatly impacted the outcome of the BAA's first-ever playoff competition. Even during the regular season, rumors swirled around Messinger's off-court life. According to Paul Birch, Messinger was "running with a bad crowd and was involved with drugs."

Here's what Johnny Norlander, the Caps' veteran center, had to say after the Chicago Stags closed out their playoff series by winning Game Six:

> We were up by six with only a couple of minutes to go, and we could taste the win. But from there until the end, the Stags made a parade to the foul line. In fact, they failed to notch a single field goal during that stretch. Just about all of the calls that sent them to the line were clearly ridiculous ones, and they were all made by the same ref—Nate Messinger. The other ref was Pat Kennedy, a guy I knew from the games he worked when I was in college. Pat was always straight as an arrow, and the two of them had reffed every single game in the series, all six of them. As we walked off the court after the final buzzer, Kennedy nodded at Messinger and said to me, "Wasn't that awful?" All I could do was sadly agree.

Four months later Norlander's sadness turned to anger. "That's when we found out that Messinger had a substantial amount of money bet on Chicago to win the series. If he'd been straight, we'd have won that Game Six then closed the Stags out back in DC. No question about it. We felt like the series, and the championship, were stolen from us by a crooked ref." Messinger was subsequently banned from ever working a BAA/NBA game again.

However, over the next few years, another Jewish ref would follow in Messinger's muddy footsteps. Moreover, dozens of Jewish players would be instrumental in bringing about the first of basketball's devastating betting scandals

Testimony: David Blatt

In June 2014 the Cleveland Cavaliers faced off against the Golden State Warriors in the NBA's championship series. The Cavs were coached by David Blatt, who had directed them to a 53-29 record during the regular season. Cleveland had cruised through the early rounds of the playoffs, but two of their starting players had suffered season-ending injuries before encountering the Warriors—Kevin Love and Kyrie Irving, both certified All-Stars. Without his high-scoring sidekicks, LeBron James wasn't at his best, and Golden State downed the Cavs in six games to win the championship.

Several leading members of national Jewish organizations were infuriated by the results. The Cavs' failure to beat the Warriors was cited as proof that all the teams in the NBA, the league's commissioner (Adam Silver, a Jew), and all the referees were blatantly anti-Semitic. "There is no other explanation for the fact that Blatt's team lost," said longtime Anti-Defamation League president Abe Foxman. "Anti-Semitism is afoot."

David Harris, the executive director of the American Jewish Committee, agreed, saying, "The referees should have given David Blatt at least a ten-point lead in each game in support of Judaism—but failed to do so," proving that the anti-anti-Semitic can be just as foolish as, and even more foolish than, the fools they normally rail against.

16

....

The Scandals of '51

In 1950 the NIT was easily the most prestigious of the collegiate postseason tournaments. And CCNY, with a record of 17-4, was one of the twelve teams selected to compete. Nat Holman's starting five comprised two blacks (Floyd Layne and Ed Warner) and three Jews (Ed Roman, Irwin Dambrot, and Al "Fatty" Roth). Moreover, the Beavers' primary substitute was Norm Mager, another Jew.

They were New York's favorite team, loved even more than the New York Giants, the New York Yankees, and even the Brooklyn Dodgers. That's because City College of New York was the third-largest university in the world, yet it had no rolling meadows, no dormitories, and no tuition. It was a subway school in the middle of Harlem, with a cement campus that was sliced by several busy streets. Its thirty-four thousand students were mostly of immigrant stock, the children of peddlers and servants, of washerwomen and pants pressers, of garment workers and streetcar conductors. They were the grandchildren of peasants and slaves. Each student needed a high school average of eighty-one to gain admittance and a ravenous intellect to stay there. They were the activists, the freethinkers, the artists, the scholars, the engineers, the social workers, and the rabble of their generation. The CCNY faculty routinely included Nobel Prize winners and professional geniuses.

Yet Nat's boys were not only the darlings of the campus, but the pride of the entire city. All of the games were played in Madison Square Garden, and after defeating San Francisco in the NIT's first round, the Beavers faced off against the powerful Kentucky Wildcats, whose illustrious coach, Adolph Rupp, once said, "I'd never coach a team with kikes and blacks."

Before the game the Kentucky players refused to shake hands with their CCNY opponents. New Yorkers of every religious, ethnic, and sports persuasion were thrilled when their hometown heroes crushed Kentucky by the lopsided score of 89–50. On the day following the game, the Kentucky state legislature passed a resolution calling for the flag on the capitol building to be flown at half-mast.

Duquesne was CCNY's next victim. Then, on March 18, the Beavers captured the NIT Championship by downing Bradley, 69–61.

Barely a week later the NCAA Tournament commenced in the same venue. After close wins against Ohio State and North Carolina State, CCNY once again bested Bradley to become the first and only team to win both the NIT and the NCAA Tournaments in a single season.

Nat and his boys were the toast of the big town. None of them were seniors, but plans were already made to form an NBA franchise composed of all the CCNY players. However, the grandiose plans, the hero worship, and the innocence of Sports America turned to disbelief, hatred, and cynicism when, on January 18, 1951, it was revealed that several members of the adored double-championship CCNY team had been doing business with gamblers. If they had played the NIT and NCAA games straight, seven players had shaved points in most of the other games in that and the current season. Further investigations revealed that a total of thirty-two players at LIU, NYU, Toledo, Bradley, Manhattan, and Kentucky had also been in league with gamblers. According to Ed Roman, one of the CCNY fixers:

> All the coaches claimed that they had no idea what was going on, but most of them were full of shit. Rupp used to curse his team out when they won but didn't cover the point spread. Clair Bee knew

at LIU and so did Nat Holman. I can remember one time when I'd been taken out of a game we were dumping and sitting right next to Holman. Bobby Sand, another Jew, was the assistant coach, and he walked over to Holman and said, "Nat, they're dumping the game." And Holman said, "Mind your own fucking business." What a laugh. The whole program was corrupt. Ed Warner was a great player, but he could barely read and yet Holman got him admitted into City College, which at the time was one of the top schools in the country. Ed got into the school only because forging high school transcripts was a widely accepted practice at City.

Alex Groza and Ralph Beard had graduated from Kentucky into the NBA, but were booted from the league in 1951 when it was revealed that they had fixed games in college. After hearing the bad news, Rupp begged for leniency. "The Chicago Black Sox threw games," he said, "but these boys only shaved points." Rupp failed to mention that Ed Curd, Lexington's most celebrated bookmaker, was a good friend. Indeed, Rupp had visited Curd in his home at least twice and had once telephoned the gambler to inquire about the point spread for a Kentucky-Alabama game. Rupp was also seen in the company of Curd at the Copacabana after a Kentucky game at Madison Square Garden. Rupp never denied the meetings, but he did swear that he had never bet on any games.

Maybe so, but here's what Dale Barnstable, one of Rupp's star players, had to say about betting on Kentucky games: "I missed a shot late in a game that we won against St. Louis and, when it was over, Rupp gave me the devil. He said that my miss had cost one of his friends five hundred dollars."

Nor did Rupp ever mention that he motivated his players with both curses and rewards. His Wildcats regularly received cash either from Rupp himself or from "boosters." The sums ranged from ten to fifty dollars, depending on how well the players performed. On the rare occasion of a loss, the ballplayers were lucky to get anything to eat.

If Rupp tried to mitigate the sins of his point-shaving players, he must have been hopping mad when he learned that two of the gamblers who worked with his boys were Eli Kaye (né Klukofsky) and Saul Feinberg, both "kikes," along with Salvatore Sollazzo, the primary fixer-in-chief and a low-level mafioso. It should also be noted that the ambitious Kaye along with Jack Rubinstein, a bookie friend from Brooklyn, were also the moneymen behind point-shaving players at Toledo.

However, most of the Jewish players and gamblers in the fix business were concentrated in New York. Among the former were LIU's Ed Gard, Jack Goldsmith, Natie Miller, and Lou Lipman. In addition to Roman, Roth, and Dambrot, who got one thousand dollars each for every crooked game), Herb Cohen was a bit player whose fee was five hundred dollars per game, as was Connie Schaff from NYU. Moreover, several players from St. John's were likewise part of the cabal, none of them Jews. But there was another fix operating.

Frank Hogan was a decent man and a devout Catholic. As such he was subjected to heavy pressure to lay off several other Catholic schools that were also heavily involved. It was common knowledge among players, coaches, bookies, and sharpsters in the metropolitan area that Cardinal Spellman took a personal interest in Hogan's investigations. "It was simple," said one local coach. "Spellman sent a retired detective to show up at Hogan's office and give him the word. That's why players from Holy Cross, DePaul, La Salle, Villanova, St. Joseph's, and St. John's went unpunished."

In addition, the coach said, Hogan's office had several recordings of telephone conversations between certain St. John's players and Eddie Gard, who was the front man for Salvatore Sollazzo. In those days the recordings were made on brittle celluloid platters. Before the recordings were transcribed, "an appointed official of the City of New York" deliberately knocked the platter to the floor, shattering it into splinters.

Moreover, whereas the incriminated players from the other local schools—who were mostly either black or Jewish—were all questioned unexpectedly, individually, and without benefit of counsel, and readily confessed, St. John's was tipped off. Consequently, their players were shepherded into Hogan's headquarters by a big-shot lawyer named Henry Urgetta and a slew of priests. Urgetta wouldn't permit the DA's men to question the St. John's players in private, and without confessions Hogan had no case. However, not only were many of the St. John's players doing business with Sollazzo, but several were also sleeping with his wife, Jeanne.

None of this was a secret. "I saw it happen many times," said a local player from a Catholic school. "As the St. John's players headed to the locker room after another disgraceful performance, scores of pissed-off bettors would be waving twenty-dollar bills and shouting, 'You guys ain't kidding nobody. The whole world knows you're all fucking Sollazzo's wife and dumping ball games.' It was ridiculous. The St. John's guys were kicking balls out of bounds and missing shots they could have made with their eyes closed. Everybody knew everything."

Because most of the altered games had been played in Madison Square Garden, Saul Streit, a Jew, was the judge who sentenced the confessed fixers—the same judge who had given the Rosenbergs the death sentence. The Jewish players were treated lightly: Al Roth, Ed Roman, and Herb Cohen were permitted to join the army instead of going to jail for six months. Irwin Dambrot received a suspended sentence because Judge Streit felt he had "realized the enormity of his misstep." A veteran of World War II, Lou Lipman likewise had his sentence suspended because of his "good war record." Connie Schaff was also the recipient of a suspended sentence. Natie Miller and Norm Mager were set free.

Of the black players involved, Floyd Layne and Leroy Smith (LIU) were also granted their freedom. But Streit directed several racial slurs at Ed Warner and Sherman White (LIU) before sentencing them to six months in prison.

For sure, the scandals were widespread, but the participation of the double-championship CCNY players broke the hearts of millions of New Yorkers. Nat Holman, however, was deemed an innocent bystander.

In any event, CCNY, LIU, and NYU downgraded their basketball programs, while Toledo, Bradley, and Kentucky continued to be among the college game's powerhouses. Overall, though, the passionate citizens of Sports America were disillusioned by college basketball, turning their attention and devotion to the pro game. Indeed, it's quite feasible that had the scandals of '51 never happened, the BAA-cum-NBA would have taken a backseat to college hoops for at least another decade.

Coincidentally or not, the scandals also marked the beginning of the end of Jewish players being routinely named to the various college All-American teams. In the 1940s twelve different Jewish players were so honored. In the decade after the scandals, only five Jews were named to All-American squads: Irv Bemoras, Illinois (1953); Lenny Rosenbluth, North Carolina (1955–57); Larry Friend, California (1957); Alan Seiden, St. John's (1958–59); and Don Goldstein, Louisville (1959). It should also be noted that only Bemoras and Rosenbluth were good enough to go on and play in the NBA—even though they were both little more than journeymen. However, in 1958, Rudy LaRusso of Dartmouth received All-American honorable mention and went on to become a five-time NBA All-Star. Indeed, "Roughhouse Rudy" was the second-best Jewish basketball player in the modern era.

Testimony: Ed Roman

Ed Roman measured six foot six and 240 pounds. He was broad beamed and thin shouldered, and even as a kid he was always bumping into things. But he was a diligent student and incredibly quick to master anything that attracted his intellect. He loved to read and spend most of his time by himself. Ed's dream was to become a research scientist.

Ed was a latecomer to athletics. He wasn't introduced to basketball until the coach at Taft High School spotted him ambling through the hallways in his sophomore year. Ed was large and self-conscious, and it was explained that basketball would do wonders for him. Make him confident. Use his bulk and his strength to great advantage.

Taft's star player was Irwin Dambrot, a great jump shooter, scorer, and future teammate of Roman's at CCNY. During Ed's sophomore year he was a full-time scrub, but he studied the game and practiced with the team and then by himself for nine hours a day. Dambrot broke his wrist the following season, and Ed was led out of the laboratory and into the center-jump circle. With his dancer's feet and uncanny one-hand shot that he flicked off the top of his forehead, Roman responded by breaking all of Dambrot's scoring records. He was All-City in his junior year and a high school All-American as a senior.

Everybody was after Ed, even St. John's. But he decided to accept a package deal from the University of Cincinnati that included tuition, board, a no-show job, fifty dollars a month for expenses, and the use of a car for both Ed and his brother. They attended classes for two days before the omnipresent Bobby Sand appeared, offering admission for him and his brother as well as a job for his father. When Ed told the Cincinnati people the bad news, they raised the ante in an effort to keep him there. But in September 1948 Ed Roman enrolled at CCNY.

He soon discovered that Holman

> was a narcissistic bastard. As a person, he typified everything that was wrong with big-time college basketball. He was very destructive to the sense of community that existed at City College. He had no business being there. There was no satisfying Holman. He undermined our confidence by riding us hard for all our mistakes. He never gave us any credit when we played well. He cursed us in his phony English accent. He screamed. He scapegoated like crazy. He didn't even know our names. He called me "Big Boy" and he called Floyd "Ed." Some of us hated the air he breathed. Sure, the money from the gamblers was wonderful, but some of us were eager to get involved with gamblers just to get even with Holman.

Norm Mager, for example. "Norm was Holman's favorite whipping boy," said Roman, "and he hated Holman with a passion. Norm even wanted to provoke Holman into a fistfight, but never did. Norm would have dumped for nothing."

Another one of Holman's players had a different opinion: "Nat was a great coach. Maybe even the greatest. Basketball is the kind of sport that demands great personal sacrifice and some of the players just couldn't reach down as far as Holman could. He never pushed any of us any harder than he pushed himself. All of his teachings were moral. I know a lot of guys hated him, but it's the easiest thing in the world to criticize a man's personality."

In any case, Roman also said, "I hate to admit it, but shaving points was a time-honored tradition at City. The choice was to go along with everybody else or to tell the authorities. Most of us were very broke and very naïve. We were this and we were that. . . . But in our hearts we knew it was wrong."

Still, Roman placed some of the blame on New York's sportswriters:

With their published point spreads and their paper bets, they helped make gambling a way of life in New York City. Almost all of the local sportswriters were Jewish and were very close to us. Sid Friedlander of the *New York Post* was a City grad and we even gave him a gold tie clasp when we won the NIT. But when everything blew open they carried on a personal vendetta against us. They were in a position to help us, to be somewhat sympathetic because we were just stupid kids who went along with what everybody else was doing, but they stepped us into the mud.

When Roman met Layne after their arrests, he said, "It's all over for us. We might as well do down to the docks and start looking for work."

But the CCNY fixers managed to survive. Ed Warner played for a few years in the Eastern League, refereed high school basketball games, and was a counselor in youth programs throughout the city. He died in 2002. Irwin Dambrot had a successful dentistry practice until his death in 2010. Floyd Lane also played in the Eastern League. He returned to CCNY as the varsity basketball coach in 1978 and is currently the junior varsity coach at George Washington High School in the Bronx.

In the mid-1970s, while researching my *Scandals of '51*, I had a brief telephone conversation with Al Roth, who sold insurance, lived in a suburb of New York, and was reputed to be a very wealthy man. "People talk about the double championship to my face," he said, "but they never mention the scandals where I can hear them. I'm sorry that my name makes people remember the scandals. A sportswriter called me recently to ask about the two Bradley games, but when the article came out, it was all about the scandals. I'm not bitter, but I can't see what good can come from any more publicity. I don't live with it anymore. I would just as soon be left alone to hope that people will forget about what happened. Sorry."

I made several other phone calls: "Yes, this is Eddie Gard . . . Who? . . . What? . . . No. No. I'm sorry. I can't help you. I'm just trying to make a living. Whatever anybody says about me is true."

On another call the phone was picked up after ringing only once. "Hello . . . ? Yes, this is him. What can I do for you? . . . Are you kidding? Why the hell would I want to talk about that stuff? My kids don't even know. I'm sorry."

Norm Mager was playing with the Baltimore Bullets when the scandal broke. After averaging 4.8 points in twenty-two games, he was immediately banished from the NBA. I caught up with him in his midtown office, where he served as an executive in a janitorial supply company.

He speared and ate his chef's salad with the efficiency of a man who knew that a lunch hour lasted only forty-five minutes. "We were guilty," he said, "but not as guilty as everybody made us out to be. There are pro boxers and baseball players who are deserters and rapists. At the time the totality of the basketball universe kept us young and immature, but I have to take the full blame on myself. I had the opportunity to refuse, and I didn't. There are no extenuating circumstances that can ease that fact or ease the pain."

He neatly nipped the corners of his mouth with a paper napkin, drained a glass of soda, and enjoyed a backhand belch. Then he finished his dessert, put down his fork, and leaned across the table. "But

I never tried to run away from it," he said. "I stayed and confronted myself even though it hurt. I've asked myself 'Why?' a million times, but I don't think I've come up with an answer that makes any sense. I try to be flexible. I know I have to forget, but I know I never really will. I have grown to feel very private about myself, about my past. And I do have the memory of my athletic accomplishments. Nothing can take that away from me. At least there's that." Norm Mager died of cancer in 2005.

Years later Ed Roman weighed 270 pounds and was periodically troubled by phlebitis. He was a psychologist in a ghetto school in Brooklyn, and he felt he could now understand why society treated a small group of postadolescents so harshly.

"The American people have a romanticized view of athletics," he said.

> They want to identify with the entire fantasy that the world of sports has come to represent. When you break a moral code that people are supposed to believe in, you are confronted with a stronger wrath than any burglar or common thief ever faces. It was also a period of rampant McCarthyism, so there were a great many self-protective reactions. All of the coaches, for example, yelled their innocence from the rooftops. We were left defenseless, and we took the rap. But I don't feel guilty anymore. The most damaging thing was that it prevented me from playing in the NBA. But the Eastern League was good for my self-esteem, and I learned to compromise. The scandals certainly changed the course of my life and interfered with my intellectual development. But I got over my bitterness and anger many years ago. I'm finally going after a PhD in psychology, and I have so many other things to get into that the scandals don't mean that much to me. Above all else, I've learned that the entire universe of sports is based on illusion.

Roman was currently helping kids in slums adjust to what the rest of the world called reality. "The coaches are still under tremendous pressure to win," he said, "and the same old double standard remains in operation. Colleges offer all kinds of illegal inducements to the players, and the kids are expected to be as pure as the driven snow. Basketball is even more commercialized than ever before, and the kids know it. I can't see that we're at all immune to another gambling scandal." Ed Roman died of leukemia in 1988.

This is what Bobby Sand had to say: "Hello? . . . Yes. . . . Speaking . . . The City College scandals? Hmmm. I don't know. That's still a touchy subject. . . . Yes. . . . Yes, I know. I was there, and I know everything that happened. I can tell you about things you'll never find in the newspapers. . . . It really doesn't sound like a good idea. . . . But wait a minute. Let me ask you a question. . . . What if I tell you everything I know for five hundred dollars?"

17

....

Murray's in the Mountains

Another casualty of the 1951 scandals was the highly competitive games between the summertime resorts in upstate New York that were owned and frequented by Jewish vacationers from New York City. Such competition attracted many of the college game's best players, but was also the scene of the gamblers' most successful recruiting endeavors.

They were variously called "the Jewish Alps" or "the Borscht Belt" and were said to be located in "Solomon County," New Yorkese for Sullivan County. The whole enterprise began after World War I, as New York Jews became increasingly prosperous. Looking to escape from the city's notoriously hot and humid summers for a weekend or even an entire week's vacation, they turned their attention to the cool Catskill Mountains, which were reached via an easy drive north along Route 17 or an even easier ride on the New York, Ontario, and Western Railway.

However, the virulent anti-Semitism in the area barred Jews from registering at the several resorts that had been catering to Gentile clients since the 1850s. Recognizing the situation, Jewish farmers in the region began taking in boarders, a highly profitable business that eventually led to the construction of bungalow colonies and then massive thousand-acre hotels like Grossinger's and the Concord.

To ensure that the guests were perpetually entertained at these hotels, young aspiring comedians were hired to keep the yuks flowing. Several of these comics, or "tummlers," went on to have very successful careers—the likes of Woody Allen, Jack Benny, Milton Berle, Sid Caesar, Jerry Lewis, Henny Youngman, and even Joan Rivers.

Here's what transpired on a typical day in a typical Catskill resort:

Good morning, ladies and germs. My name is Buster Babich, and I'm your host and social director here at Murray's in the Mountains. I'll tell a few jokes, sing a few songs, and . . . Wait a minute. Wait a minute. . . . What are you looking, darling? I'm the social director, not your waiter. Furschtast Yiddish, darling? . . . Ha! Can my bubba make meintzer? Is the Pope Catholic? . . . I'm your host, darling. I'm the tummler. And for you I've got some special tummling already in mind. But listen, everybody. They're already wheeling out the pastry table. Another exclusive feature of Murray's in the Mountains. So let me tell you what we have planned for today, and let me get the hell out of here before I get trampled. . . . In a half hour, we'll have a hilarious game of Dirty Simon Sez out on the pool deck with yours truly doing the sezzing. . . . At eleven o'clock, there's a shuffleboard tournament, also at the pool. There's a cha-cha lesson at noon. . . . Soon, darling. Relax. You're drooling all over your mink coat. . . . Then there's mah-jongg instruction. . . . It's almost ready, everybody. Sit down a second. Hold your horses. . . . There's a basketball game at eight o'clock with the bellhops and the kitchen boys playing the Grossinger's All-Stars. There's also a betting pool in case anybody's interested. . . . There's a Ping . . . Ladies and gentlemen! Presenting ten yards of confectionery delights! The Murray's in the Mountains world-famous Viennese Table is now OPEN! Forget your diet, enjoy yourselves, and I'll see you later.

In the early 1930s, the owner of a Catskill resort learned that several members of the staff were college basketball players from New York. The players periodically organized their own games to stay in shape, and the owner, quick to see the possibility of an added attraction, encouraged the guests to watch them play.

The idea caught on, and within a few years virtually all of the area's two hundred hotels were fielding liveried basketball teams. Ballplayers from all over the country jumped at the chance to earn some extra money, have a good time, and play some very competitive ball. Some of the players applied for the jobs by letter, and some simply appeared in May when the hiring was done. But most of them were placed by their college coaches, who arranged for as many of their own players as possible to work and play at the same hotel.

Oftentimes, professional players would seek summer-long employment to augment their paltry salaries, stay in shape, or just have some fun. Or they might show up for a few days, be treated royally, and be advertised in the New York newspapers as an extra on-court attraction to draw new customers.

The waiters, busboys, and bellhops had the most difficult jobs and made the most money. Their average salary was forty dollars a month, and they picked up anywhere from five hundred to a thousand dollars in tips. There were also soft jobs available on the athletic staff, teaching tennis and swimming and organizing the guests into games of softball. The easier jobs paid only three hundred dollars for the summer, and there were never any tips. But the athletic staff could sleep through breakfast, and they didn't have to work at all when it rained. Another resort attraction for these young men was the scads of lonely and eager young ladies whose husbands worked in the city and vacationed only on weekends.

There were some resorts, however, where the ballplayers were expected to do the same amount of work as the other hired hands. "Guests like to watch basketball games," one hotel owner explained, "but they love to eat. If the best basketball player in the world is slow with the roast beef, or lets the coffee get cold, then I lose a paying customer."

The hotel teams usually played two games a week and practiced every day. There were no actual leagues, no standings, and no winner at the end of the season. But basketball games featuring the likes of Bob Cousy, Alex Groza, and George Mikan provided wonderful entertainment for a summer's evening. The ball games also served to keep the guests and their money on the hotel premises. There were few tummlers who dared to announce "away" games.

In addition to salaries and tips, the ballplayers had another substantial source of income: a hat would be passed around the stands, and guests could pick a number for a dollar. Ed Roman explained:

> It was a betting pool to match the total number of points scored in the ball game. We used to split the pot with the winner and pocket an extra ten or fifteen dollars every time we played. But the fix was working even in the summertime. Sometimes, if one of us had a friend or a relative at the game, we'd find out his number and make sure he was the winner. When nobody we knew well enough to control the scoring was on hand, we'd make sure that the chef's number would be the winner. Then we'd eat like kings for a week.

In any given summer, there were perhaps five hundred varsity basketball players employed in the Jewish Alps. Among them were either current or former players like Eddie Gard (LIU) and Jackie Goldsmith (NYU), plus players from Manhattan College and St. John's—guys who were recruiting agents for gamblers and bookies.

After the betting scandals were revealed, the Catskill resorts (along with Madison Square Garden) came under attack. Phog Allen, the revered coach at Kansas, said, "The boys who participate in the resort hotel games during the summer months are thrown into an environment which cannot help but breed the evil which more and more is coming to light."

Newspaper columnists all over the country joined the attack. The resort teams were "subterfuges for professionalism." In the Catskills, "The seeds are planted by the wily fixers for future harvests." The "softening-up process" began in the Borscht Belt.

Even Nat Holman got into the act. "The hotel teams," he said, "are schools of crime. And since playing for these hotel teams may have a bad influence on the boys, we at CCNY have decided not to allow their participation there. I've told the boys that if they disobey this new regulation, they'll be dropped from the squad." Many other colleges followed suit.

Testimony: Charley Rosen

I played against Ed Roman once, and once was enough. My coach at Hunter College was Mike Fleischer, who had been a classmate and close friend of the infamous CCNY fixers. One of Coach's best pals was Ed Roman, so on one memorable occasion just prior to my sophomore season, Roman showed up at the Hunter gym. The idea was for him to tutor me in the theories and practices of pivot play. Footwork. Balance. Boxing out. The works.

We then played some one-on-one, wherein I hoped to demonstrate how much of his instruction I had absorbed. After I missed a midrange jumper, I tried to bully my way around Roman's wide body and attack the offensive board. So, as per his teaching, I executed a quick bang to freeze him, and then I hooked him with my left arm, followed by a half spin, and I thought I was there.

All at once the lights went out. Out of nowhere, his elbow had blasted the middle of my face into a red, pulpy mess. Roman offered no apology. Instead, he simply walked out of the gym. I wondered then (and since) what that particular lesson was all about. Perhaps it was just a manifestation of his lingering bitterness. Of his anger? His guilt? But why take it out on me?

Anyway, Coach Fleischer drove me to Fordham Hospital, where a doctor inserted two metal rods into my collapsed nasal passages and, with one blood-soaked and agonizing yank, realigned the broken bone into at least a semblance of its original position.

According to Coach, the blood, the swelling, and the subsequent black eyes were all badges of honor. I was now a bona fide "big man," theoretically unafraid to stick my face into the rebounding scrums in the shadow of the basket.

Coach further consoled me by saying that a busted nose was much preferable to a sprained ankle, because the latter would prevent me from playing. "Don't worry," he added. "Before you're through, you'll break a lot of other guys' noses!" Which—either thanks or no thanks to Ed Roman—I never did.

18

············

If It's Broken, Keep Fixing It

In 1948 the BAA had merged with the NBL to form the NBA. Yet the ghost of Nate Messinger continued to haunt the new league. The latest crooked referee was Sol Levy, another Jew. The continuing investigation into the college fixes by Vincent O'Connor, an assistant district attorney in Manhattan, discovered that Levy had conspired with the same Salvatore Sollazzo who bankrolled most of the point shavers in New York to alter the outcome of six NBA games in 1950. For payments that varied between four and nine hundred dollars, Levy made certain that previously specified players were prematurely fouled out of those games. Levy swore he was innocent and that he had been framed by Eddie Gard. An NBA vet at the time said this: "Levy wasn't the only ref doing business, not by a long shot. A ref named Chuck Soladare told me face-to-face that he was betting on ball games. The difference was that Chuck and a bunch of other refs would only bet on games they weren't personally working."

In any event, Levy was tried before a three-judge panel and was voted guilty by a margin of two to one. The dissenting judge said that deliberately fouling out basketball players was not a punishable offense. The conviction was eventually overturned by a higher court, which held that Levy was a paid independent contractor and that the bribery laws applied only to gamblers and athletes. Levy then swore that this final ruling totally exonerated him.

Yet even with the widespread college scandals perpetually in the news, and even with Sol Levy banished from the NBA, there was worse to come in both the college and the pro games. And as before there were several Jews at the heart of these subsequent conspiracies.

A Sephardic Jew, Jacob "Jack" Molinas was a great basketball player and a master game fixer, with both of these qualities becoming evident when he was in high school. During the course of his career at Stuyvesant High School, Molinas became acquainted with Joe Hacken, a small-time but very ambitious Jewish bookie who lived in the same Bronx neighborhood. By his senior year the six-foot-six, 180-pound Molinas was already being hailed as the greatest high school basketball player New York City had ever produced. In the parlance of those days, he could "run like a deer." He could also score with driving hook shots and a soft one-handed push shot. Adhesive hands and quick hops also made Molinas an excellent rebounder. During that 1948–49 season Molinas arranged with Hacken to alter the winning margins of several of Stuyvesant's games. For Molinas, the financial payoffs were small but satisfying.

Then on March 19, 1949, Molinas earned his biggest bribe, when Stuyvesant played Lincoln High School in Madison Square Garden for the Public School Athletic League championship. Before the game Molinas proudly announced to his friends that he was going to get eight hundred dollars from a guy named Joe Hacken to throw the game. Whereas Molinas had previously been averaging twenty-eight points per game, he scored a mere twelve—and badly missed a free throw that would have tied the game with eight seconds left to play.

Molinas's next stop was Columbia University, where he continued to work with Hacken in certain games and play brilliantly otherwise. Indeed, Molinas had mastered his game plan to such a degree that he was able to score thirty-nine points while deliberately blowing a game against Holy Cross.

In any event, his obvious talent made him a first-round draft pick (fifth overall) of the NBA's Fort Wayne Pistons. After a few games in his rookie season of 1953–54, Molinas was averaging fourteen points and seven rebounds per game and was delighted when several of his new teammates invited him to join their own point-shaving coterie.

George Mikan was the league's highest-paid player, earning twelve thousand dollars annually from the Minneapolis Lakers. Bob Cousy of the Boston Celtics and Syracuse's Dolph Schayes each made an estimated seven thousand dollars. According to a former NBAer who played from 1949 to 1953:

> All the rest of us got paid about thirty-five hundred bucks plus seven bucks a day for meal money on the road. Believe me, it wasn't easy if you had to live on that kind of money, especially if you had a wife and kids. Lookit, you had to pay rent or mortgage payments on your home, plus rent for an apartment in the city where you played. That's why a lot of good players couldn't afford to play in the NBA. At the same time, a lot of us had no other choice. There were no other career options available to us. We had to make a living, you know? And that's why so many NBA players in the late forties and early fifties were doing business.

Like who? "Like almost all the players on the Baltimore Bullets," said one veteran of that team (whose testimony was corroborated by other veterans of what is called "the Pioneer Era").

> There was one player on another team, a big man, who occasionally played to lose. When his teammates figured out what he was doing they were pissed. Oh, shit. There he goes again. Instead of throwing him catchable passes in the pivot, they'd throw passes at his ankles just to make him look clumsy. There was another big-time player, a guard, who would signal to the gamblers that he

was on the take by taking a long running hook shot the first time he touched the ball. Who else? A bunch of guys on the Knicks, especially the players who came from New York.

Whitey Von Nieda, who played three NBA seasons with the old Tri-Cities Blackhawks, recalled several teammates who studied the point spreads that were printed in the newspapers "like other guys studied the Bible."

Commissioner Podoloff was no fool. Private investigators he had hired turned up conclusive proof that the pro game was not on the level. He demanded that the owner of a team in the Eastern Conference release a player who was in league with gamblers—or else the player's name and misdeeds would be made public. The owner refused Podoloff's demand and threatened to fold his franchise if the player's name was released to the press. Rather than risk one of the NBA's prime-time teams dropping out, Podoloff did nothing.

Still, the commissioner had to do something. Somebody had to take the fall, to set an example, if nothing else. And Podoloff and his advisers settled on Jack Molinas. He was a rookie from an Ivy League school, and he played for one of the smallest media markets in the NBA. Even though Molinas had been named to participate in the upcoming 1984 All-Star Game, he was far from being one of the league's most prominent players.

In order to protect the NBA's legitimacy, Podoloff would never give any indication that so many games were not on the up-and-up. If he did, the entire league would collapse before the newspaper headlines were dry. So the charge against Molinas dealt with his having bet on several of the Pistons' games—but only on Fort Wayne to win. That this was a bald-faced lie was attested to by several players.

Zeke Sinicola was a little-used sub for the Pistons and Molinas's roommate on the road. "I wasn't stupid," Sinicola said, "so I knew exactly what was going on. But I wasn't in any way interested in dumping games because I understood what the consequences were. And for me, playing professional basketball was like playing out a dream. The point is that the dream was strong for me, but it wasn't as strong for Jack, and that's why he got fucked up."

Irv Bemoras was a benchwarmer with the Milwaukee Hawks and had been a teammate of Molinas during an extended exhibition tour matching the NBA champion Minneapolis Lakers against the College All-Stars. Bemoras remembered a game in which the Pistons beat the last-place Hawks but failed to cover the point spread. "There was Jack on the free throw line late in the game," said Bemoras, "and he shot the ball like he was heaving a shot put. Bang! The ball slammed against the backboard. And I yelled out, 'Jack, what's going on?' He just shrugged and flashed me one of his 'don't worry' smiles. It was clear that there was something improper happening and I remember being shocked. After the game, when I asked him about it again, he giggled like a little boy, shrugged his shoulders, and said nothing."

According to another contemporary player, Bill Tosheff, "The word was definitely out around the NBA that several of the Fort Wayne players were occasionally throwing games away." Since gambling on games in any way, shape, or form was illegal, Podoloff banished Molinas from the NBA.

But if Molinas was banned from the pros, he simply turned his attention to the college game. With Molinas out, there were only four Jewish players left in the NBA—and Dolph Schayes still reigned supreme.

Testimony: Dolph Schayes

Growing up, Dolph Schayes was my idol. That's because, like me, he was from the Bronx, was six foot eight, and was Jewish. I saw him play live with my GO (General Organization) pass that was made available to all high school students in New York City for some modest fee that I can't recall. But I do remember that the pass allowed me entrance into any and all events at Madison Square Garden for only twelve cents. I also saw Schayes play dozens of times on TV.

When I practiced shooting one-on-none in the schoolyard, I fancied that I was Dolph Schayes. I even tried to perfect his deadly high-arcing, two-handed set shot that he released from over his head. But once I was old enough to hoop in high school, the game had changed. Set shooters were ridiculed, one-handed push shots were barely tolerated, and jump shots were "in."

In addition to Dolph's extraordinary scoring and rebounding feats, and his participation in twelve consecutive All-Star Games, I was unduly impressed by how, in 1951, he adjusted his game plan after suffering what was called "an incomplete fracture of a small bone in his right wrist." A "lightweight cast and rubberized cover" was applied to the injury, and Schayes was allowed to play. With his trademark set shot in temporary abeyance, he simply used his not-so-lightweight cast as a battering ram and concentrated on driving and blasting his way to the basket and shooting with his off hand. He played this way for six weeks until the cast was removed. Schayes claimed the injury was a blessing in disguise, since it forced him to develop shots, passes, and dribbling with his theretofore barely used left hand. I almost wished that I would somehow suffer a similar injury—but to my left hand—so I could duplicate my hero's legal mayhem.

After my freshman year at Hunter College, I was a counselor at Camp Walden, an upstate summer camp that was owned by Schayes— and that's when I first made a personal connection with him. It was a brief meeting, to be sure. He shook my hand, told me to practice hard and often, wished me luck, and halfheartedly agreed to meet me on the basketball court to give me "a few pointers." Unfortunately, he spent a few hours with the camp's accountant and then made a hasty exit.

I encountered him again many years later at Kutsher's Hotel, a fancy resort in the Catskill Mountains. I was there to interview Darryl Dawkins for a profile that would appear in *Sport Magazine*. Dawkins was there—along with numerous other NBA players—to compete in the annual Maurice Stokes Games. This was a charity event designed to raise funds necessary to provide health care for Stokes, an All-Star player who had suffered severe brain damage after being knocked to the floor during a ball game.

Schayes was there to serve as the honorary coach of a team of retired NBA players who would face a similar team in another exhibition contest. However, only four players on his team were on hand during the pregame warm-ups.

In any event, Schayes invited me to sit beside him on the bench while his abbreviated squad rehearsed their layups. We reminisced about playing ball in the Creston Avenue schoolyard, where the only games permitted were three-on-three, two-on-two, and one-on-one. We both laughed at how easily the resident star of that game—Jack Molinas—had so easily embarrassed both of us, Dolph in the late 1940s and early '50s, me in the early '60s. "Jack was arrogant, and as crooked as the baskets were in the schoolyard," Dolph said. "But he was one of the greatest players I ever faced."

Meanwhile, game time was getting closer. Dolph quickly checked out my standard-issue sneakers and then said, "I see you're wearing Chuck Taylor's. Are you in any kind of shape?"

Imagine my enthusiasm as I said, "Absolutely!"

"Okay, then. Why don't you start the game until some other guys get here?"

"Yes! Yes! Thank you!"

So I tightened my sneaks, gave Dolph my wallet to hold, and prepared to do battle with Zelmo Beaty, the roughest-toughest player of his generation. How intimidating was Z? So much so that opposing centers were unable to sleep the night before they played against him. Yet a beating at the hands and elbows of Z would be a small price to play for actually . . .

Uh-oh. Before I had a chance to get up from my seat, Jumpin' Johnny Green ambled into the gym. Dolph was gracious enough to shrug and say, "I'm sorry, Charley. Maybe next time. But, hey. Why don't you hang around in case somebody twists an ankle or gets a cramp or something?" I did, but I had to settle for handing towels to Schayes's players during time-outs.

The next—and last—time I encountered Dolph was at the Naismith Hall of Fame back in early September 2007. For me, the occasion was a personal invitation and a front-row seat to witness Phil Jackson's induction. Dolph was there to be introduced the next morning and make a brief talk along with all the other surviving Hall of Fame members.

I was totally surprised and astounded when Phil, in his acceptance speech, cited my three-year stint as his assistant coach with the CBA's Albany Patroons as being a significant contribution to his later successes coaching in the NBA. I never thought that was the case (and still don't), but I was thrilled.

The next morning all those still present gathered for an informal buffet breakfast. Since our last encounter at Kutsher's, I had done a few phone interviews with Dolph in connection with various other pieces I'd written for other publications. So we found each other in the loose crowd and caught each other up on our current days and ways. We shook hands and patted each other's backs when the signal came for the official ceremonies to commence. And Dolph laughed as he said these last words to me: "Charley, if you give me a hundred dollars, I'll also mention your name."

On December 10, 2015, at the age of eighty-seven, Dolph Schayes succumbed to a six-month battle with cancer. Goodbye, Dolph. RIP. Thanks for the almost-run. And, most important, thanks for being an even better human being than you were a player.

19

....

David Beats Goliath Again

Wilt Chamberlain was simply one of the greatest all-around athletes ever. As a seven-foot-one, 245-pound preteen in Philadelphia, he ran the 440-yard dash in forty-nine seconds and high-jumped six feet, six inches. Later at the University of Kansas, he ran a 100-yard dash in a fraction over ten seconds, reached fifty-six feet in the shot put, from a standing start made a twenty-two-foot broad jump, and in the hop-skip-and-jump (now called the triple jump) his best distance was forty-five feet, nine inches. Moreover, he was a pretty good basketball player.

He was so good that the NCAA had to institute a pair of anti-Wilt rules. That's because as a high school player he used to shoot his free throws in a highly unusual manner—starting several feet behind the stripe and then jumping high and far enough to dunk the ball before he landed. Also, on under-in-bounds plays, the ball was thrown over the backboard so that Chamberlain was able to catch it and execute another slam-jam.

Both of his favorite ploys were outlawed by the time Chamberlain was eligible to play varsity ball for the Jayhawks in the 1956–57 season. Routinely faced with double- and triple-teaming, as well as box-and-one and triangle-and-two gimmick defenses, Chamberlain still averaged 29.6 points and 18.9 rebounds in leading the Jayhawks to a 20-2 record and an invite to the 1957 NCAA Tournament. No wonder Chamberlain was a unanimous selection on both the Associated Press and the United Press International All-American teams.

Even so, there were many who believed that Chamberlain was merely a freak. As such numerous sportswriters denigrated and even ridiculed his accomplishments. Chamberlain's reaction was this: "Nobody roots for Goliath."

Led by the irresistible Chamberlain, Kansas breezed through the Western Regionals, beating Southern Methodist University (SMU), Oklahoma City, and San Francisco by an average of more than 17 points per game. In the championship game the number-two-ranked Jayhawks faced off against the top-ranked and undefeated North Carolina Tar Heels. North Carolina was led by their own All-American, six-foot-five, Bronx-born Lennie Rosenbluth, an energetic rebounder and high-octane scorer who had averaged 28 points per game.

The Tar Heels' path to the championship game was a difficult one. After trouncing Yale, Canisius, and Syracuse, North Carolina needed three overtime periods the night before to defeat Michigan State. The Kansas–North Carolina matchup was billed as being the latest "Game of the Century." And, indeed, it was a well-remembered classic.

Rosenbluth tallied 20 points, even though he fouled out in the game's thirty-eighth minute. Chamberlain was, once again, double- and often triple-teamed and was limited to only six field goals and 23 total points as the Tar Heels prevailed 54–53 in another triple-overtime contest.

After that season Rosenbluth received many honors, the most significant being his beating out Chamberlain for the College Player of the Year. Rosenbluth was subsequently hailed from coast to coast as the ultimate underdog hero. Not surprisingly, the Jewish citizens of Sports America simply idolized him. And to this day Lennie Rosenbluth joins the likes of Billy Cunningham, Bob McAdoo, James Worthy, Walter Davis, and Michael Jordan as legendary figures in Chapel Hill.

In the 1957 draft the Philadelphia Warriors made Rosenbluth the sixth overall selection in what was a down year for college talent.

Chosen ahead of Rosenbluth were Rod Hundley, Charlie Tyra, Jim Krebs, Win Wilfong, and Brendan McCann—with only "Hot Rod" enjoying any notable success in the NBA. However, the one player who turned out to be a brilliant pro was tabbed two slots after Rosenbluth—Sam Jones.

It turned out, though, that Rosenbluth's pro career was short (1957–59) and not so sweet (4.2 points per game). Rosenbluth has been named to the Jewish Sports Hall of Fame. However, and with no disrespect intended, because of his stupendous career at North Carolina, Rosenbluth is at least as deserving to be enshrined at the Naismith Hall of Fame as Nancy Lieberman, Sam Balter, and Ed Wachter—three other Jewish players who have been so honored.

With Rosenbluth a bust, the second-best Jewish player in the NBA at the time was Rudy LaRusso, another Brooklyn-born and -bred player. LaRusso's mother was Jewish, his father was Italian, and his skills were honed by Harry "Jammy" Moscowitz, the legendary coach at James Madison High School. From there the six-foot-eight, 230-pound LaRusso went on to set numerous scoring and rebounding records at Dartmouth. In the 1959 draft the Minneapolis Lakers picked LaRusso in the second round (tenth pick overall), and he went on to average 16.9 points and 10.2 rebounds, while being named to five All-Star Games over the course of his eleven-year NBA career.

LaRusso was renowned for his rebounding, his defense, and his all-around toughness. But early in the 1962–63 season he tallied 50 points against the St. Louis Hawks, the most points a Jewish player has ever scored in an NBA game. Like Rosenbluth, Rudy LaRusso absolutely deserves admittance into the Naismith Hall of Fame.

Testimony: Lennie Rosenbluth

Here's more about and from Lennie Rosenbluth: "My mother's parents were immigrants from Hungary, my father's from Russia, and my grandparents spoke Yiddish and very little English." Rosenbluth's parents were not at all religious, "yet we celebrated all the Jewish holidays so I could stay out of school. And yes, I was bar mitzvahed, but in a ceremony at home, not in a synagogue."

He attended James Monroe High School, where he became an all-city selection by his junior year. "I first learned how to play the game in parks and schoolyards all over the Bronx. I had every shot from two-hand sets to hooks, from jumpers to one-handers. I could play inside and outside. And, even though I weighed only 175 pounds, I was a very aggressive rebounder. Plus, I always played with all my might, because there were dozens of guys waiting for 'next,' 'after next,' and so on. That meant if you lost one of those games, you had to stand around for another hour before you could get back on the court again."

Yet Rosenbluth's game took a quantum jump when, in the summer after his sophomore year, he began working and playing at various resort hotels in the Catskills. "Going against guys who were stars in college and in the NBA improved my skills quickly and dramatically."

When Rosenbluth had an outstanding outing against a team from Kutsher's Hotel that was coached by Red Auerbach, a sequence was initiated that eventually led him to the University of North Carolina (UNC). "In those days," says Rosenthal, "the school year in New York began immediately after Labor Day. But instead of going back to Monroe, I accepted Auerbach's invitation to come up to Boston and work out with the Celtics. This was in September 1951, so I missed the first two weeks of school to play with the Celtics. Of course, this was illegal, but there were lots of things done in those days that weren't kosher."

After Rosenbluth more than held his own against Auerbach's pros, he was encouraged to come to see the Celtics play whenever they appeared in Madison Square Garden. "I told him that I couldn't afford tickets, so Auerbach put me on what was called 'the Gate List.' This allowed all the college players in New York free admission to NBA games. But since we were not given any seats, we just wandered around during the games."

However, Rosenbluth was spotted by Hy Gotkin, a Jewish hooper-about-town who had starred at St. John's in the early 1940s and then in the American Basketball League. Gotkin, who numbered Frank McGuire, the current coach at St. John's, among his buddies, found a seat for Rosenbluth that was adjacent to his. Before long McGuire showed up and offered Rosenbluth a full scholarship to St. John's. "I turned him down because I had to take the subway to get from my home to high school, and I didn't want to have to do the same thing to get to college."

Even so, Rosenbluth liked and admired McGuire. "He never yelled at or embarrassed a player who had made a bad mistake. In fact, he'd wait until the next dead ball to take the guy out of the game, then go over and speak to him quietly when he got to the bench."

Another reason for Rosenbluth's turning down McGuire was that Everett Case at North Carolina State was actively recruiting him. So eager was Case to signing Rosenbluth that he invited the high school senior to come to MSG and scrimmage with the Wolfpack whenever they were in town. "I had no trouble whatsoever scoring against NC State's varsity players."

Then in April 1952 Rosenbluth paid a visit to NC State's campus in Raleigh. "When I got there, Case wanted me to work out with his team. My high school season had ended about a month before, so I was very much out of shape. And I didn't have any sneakers or work-out gear with me. But Case insisted. He suited me up with practice shorts and jersey and a pair of new sneakers, and I played. Trouble was, my feet quickly developed painful blisters, and I was so out of shape that every muscle in my body began to ache. The result was that I played very poorly."

Subsequently, and despite the fact that Rosenbluth had torn up Case's players during scrimmages back at MSG, the scholarship offer was rescinded.

I couldn't believe it! And when I got back to New York, McGuire got in touch and asked me what had happened at NC State. Then he told me a secret. Even after leading St. John's to the championship game of the 1952 NCAA Tournament, he was going to leave New York and find a job elsewhere. I guess things were pretty hot around the city after the CCNY, NYU, and LIU betting scandals broke out. Anyway, McGuire said he didn't know where he'd wind up, but that wherever it might be, he needed me to come with him and start a powerhouse program. I agreed. And that's how both of us came to UNC.

Under McGuire's game plan, the Tar Heels' offense was simple: "Get the ball to me and let me do whatever I wanted to do."

Rosenbluth responded by being named an All-American in both his junior and then his senior seasons. "We had terrific teams. Pete Brennan, Tommy Kearns, Ken Rosemond, and Joe Quigg were the other starters, and we could all shoot, score in the low post, and rebound like crazy." In fact, the four career leaders in rebounds-per-game average at North Carolina are still Billy Cunningham (15.9), Doug Moe (10.6), Pete Brennan (10.5), and Rosenbluth (10.4).

"In addition, none of us were afraid to take the last win-or-lose shot. Rosemond was a local guy from Hillsboro. The rest of the starters plus Bob Cunningham, Stan Groll, Bob Young, and Bill Hathaway were all from New York, so we had great fun playing and hanging out together."

Of course, Rosenbluth's college career peaked with the NCAA Championship game against Chamberlain and his University of Kansas playmates. "Here's what Coach McGuire told us before that game: 'There's no way Kansas can beat us, but Wilt certainly can.' So we concentrated on preventing Chamberlain from touching the ball by simply triple-teaming him with one player in back of him, one player fronting him, and one player up against his left shoulder, so, even if he did catch an entry pass, he couldn't take a right-handed dribble into the middle." The other two UNC defenders played a one-one zone, with one player covering whoever had the ball and the other player dropping off into the paint.

"What happened was that Chamberlain's teammates were so

programmed to get the ball in to him that they were hesitant to dribble and even more hesitant to shoot open shots. They also came out playing a box-and-one defense against me, which made no sense, since Wilt was always there to protect the rim. Anyway, we were ahead 11–2 when they finally went to a standard two-one-two zone defense."

Decades before the installation of the shot clock in college ball, both teams were extremely careful and deliberate on offense. Then Rosenbluth fouled out with one minute and thirty seconds left in regulation. "Both teams out-and-out froze the ball throughout the initial five-minute overtime. We each scored only two points, with Kansas's scores coming on a pair of free throws by Chamberlain. Then nobody scored in the second overtime. Can you imagine Wilt Chamberlain scoring only two points in ten minutes of play?"

As the third overtime period crawled to the finish line, Kansas was ahead 53–52 with only six seconds remaining. "That's when Quigg got fouled on a drive and made both of his free throws. They called a time-out and discussed their obvious last-gasp strategy, to get the ball in to Chamberlain. But Ron Lonesky underthrew the pass, and it was tipped away. Quigg came up with the loose ball and threw it high up into the rafters. Before the ball landed, the game was over and we were the champs!"

Yet Rosenbluth's subsequent career with the Philadelphia Warriors wasn't nearly as joyful. "The team had lots of talent: Paul Arizin, Neil Johnston, Woody Sauldsberry . . . But Paul Seymour was the coach, and he never told me what my role was supposed to be. I never knew if he wanted me to shoot or pass or give Arizin a rest or whatever. So I mostly sat on the bench for two years. After my contract was up, they wanted me to return, but I quit. I mean, to me, playing basketball is all about having fun. And that's certainly not what I was experiencing in Philadelphia."

After the NBA Rosenbluth played a couple of games in a weekend minor league—the Eastern League. But he was living in New Jersey at the time, and driving to so many games played in so many distant cities wasn't worth the effort.

Soon enough, he returned to North Carolina, where he taught American history and coached the varsity team at Wilson High School. "This was in 1962, and my salary was thirty-seven hundred dollars for teaching plus five hundred dollars for coaching. In my first year as a coach, we lost every game but had fun. The second year we won our first eight games. Then our best player got the measles, and we didn't win again. And it was still fun."

Next stop was Coral Gables High School, where, for the same duties, Rosenbluth was paid fifty-two hundred dollars. "I'd met my wife Pat back in college, and she was also a teacher. It was a good life for both of us that lasted almost twenty years . . . until she was diagnosed with cancer." When her condition failed to improve, Rosenbluth decided to move back to Chapel Hill. "That was because the medical facilities were better there. But it was too late. We had been married for fifty-three years when Pat passed away in 2010." Rosenbluth then decided that there was no reason to leave Chapel Hill.

One year later Rosenbluth remarried. "Dianne and I will be celebrating our fifth anniversary in a couple of weeks. And life is fun again."

What occupies his time these days? "At age eighty-three, not much. We do some traveling. Up to New York for a few days to see two or three Broadway shows. Down to Florida to visit with my two children, Steve and Beth, and my six grandchildren."

Five of his former UNC teammates are still alive, and they still keep in touch and occasionally visit. "I also wait for UNC's basketball and football seasons to begin. I have good seats for all of the home games, and I never miss one. Although I must admit, at my age, and with my aching knees and an aching back, the basketball court looks like it's a mile long."

At this stage of his days and ways, Lennie Rosenbluth, who was arguably the best Jewish player in the history of modern-day college basketball, is still having fun. "I have lots of good friends, a loving family, so there's no reason for me not to be happy."

20

....

Molinas Redux

After being accepted into Brooklyn College Law School, Jack Molinas tried to overturn the NBA's banishment ruling by saying if he was clean enough for one, he should be clean enough for the other. But Podoloff was adamant.

To satisfy his Basketball Jones, Molinas played in the Eastern League, a weekend outfit that provided top-notch competition. Among the best players were several convicted fixers—Sherman White from LIU and Ed Roman, Floyd Layne, and Ed Warner late of CCNY's double-championship team.

Hubie Brown was destined to become a Hall of Fame coach in the NBA, but after graduating from Niagara, he also spent some time in the Eastern League. "Remember," said Brown, "there were only eight teams in the NBA and only ten players on each team. That adds up to eighty players. Guys played in the Eastern League because there was no place else for them to play. I'm telling you the truth here, that many of the guys in the Eastern League would be NBA All-Stars if they played today."

One important difference between the EL and the NBA was that no point spreads were printed in any of the area's newspapers. That's why all the games were on the level. "The Eastern League was a hell of a league," Brown added. "Everybody played a cerebral kind of game with a lot of motion. It was a form of a passing game before anybody gave it a name. A lot of the old guys, especially those from the Northeast, called it Jew basketball."

In the 1955–56 EL season Molinas averaged 27.3 points per game to lead the league in scoring and was named the Most Valuable Player—all this for a measly $150 a game. But there were other games in other venues that soon proved to be much more profitable for him. These were played in the Catskills, where interresort basketball games had gradually been revived. Molinas's aim here was to start a new career: instead of a point shaver, he set out to become a master fixer. As ever, Joe Hacken was his trusty aide, while Aaron Wagman and Joe Green were added as the first of many subcontractors.

Molinas would slip several potential recruits a few bucks after a game and even let some of them borrow his car. *Hey, how could someone who was such a good player and such a generous guy be untrustworthy?* And when Molinas finally made his pitch—easy money, everybody's doing it, and you won't even have to dump any games—there were few starry-eyed high school and college kids who could turn him down.

Within a few years his stable of point shavers had expanded to include dozens of varsity players plus blue-chip high school and freshman players who agreed to do business with him once they became eligible to play varsity ball.

In time his operation grew so large that he needed some big-time money at his disposal. Molinas's first connection was with Dave Goldberg, a prosperous bookie who was connected with the Mafia. According to their deal, Molinas would provide Goldberg and his associates with the players he controlled and the games they should bet. In addition to the money Molinas made on his own bets, Goldberg also paid him $150 for every winner he provided.

The collaboration was so successful that Molinas and Goldberg soon formed similar associations with every significant gambling operation in the United States, Canada, and Mexico. Not only did Molinas get his share of the profits, but all of his expenses were covered.

Instead of slipping a player a $20 bill, he could now distribute $100 at a time and treat recruits and their girlfriends to dinners at high-priced restaurants—all for the purpose of making them feel obligated to Molinas. This went on for several years, to the point where Molinas controlled as many as twenty college games on any one night. Subsequently, he was able to deal with Goldberg's superiors, particularly Norman Rosenthal, who worked out of Chicago, and increase his payoffs.

But then Molinas got greedy. He started giving Rosenthal inflated point spreads. If, for example, the true spread was Team A minus three and a half points, Molinas would tell Rosenthal it was six and a half. Then Molinas would keep the money Rosenthal gave him to bet on Team A, wager his own money on Team A to win by four to six points, make the proper arrangements with the key players on Team A—and pocket as much as $10,000 on a single game. To ensure that these schemes worked, Molinas had to branch out and lure several college referees onto his payroll.

Of course, Molinas had to carefully pick his games and make sure that Rosenthal and his group would make high-end profits on several other fixed games played the same night. Besides, if Molinas could produce winners in 70 percent of the games he touted, then nobody had a beef. The name that Molinas playfully gave his organization was Fixers Incorporated.

But then Wagman made a critical mistake. On September 4, 1960, Wagman attempted to bribe a University of Florida football player, fullback John McBeth, to fix a game. McBeth not only resisted but informed his coach, who passed the information on to the local police. Wagman was quickly arrested, and it was inevitable that, later rather than sooner, the trail of evidence, tapped telephones, and confessions by remorseful players would eventually lead to Jack Molinas.

Meanwhile, after laying low for a few weeks, Molinas resumed business as usual. The only difference was that the Mafia moneymen behind Rosenthal discovered that Molinas was cheating them. They summoned him to Chicago, ostensibly to give him a per-game raise. But Molinas was surprised when he was faced with his underhanded dealings. When a professional goon proceeded to hold him by his feet while Molinas was dangled from the window on the eighth floor of the hotel, Molinas vowed he'd be straight as an arrow forevermore. Under the circumstances, this was easy for him to say, but it was a vow he couldn't possibly fulfill.

Indeed, after a few more of his dishonest dealings, five more goons were sent to find Molinas, surround him, and then beat him to a pulp. However, by executing a few head fakes, a strategic shoulder bump, and a life-or-death fast break, Molinas made his getaway.

By now the cops were on to him. Molinas could tell by the funny noises he heard when he made telephone calls at his usual location—a public phone bank near his childhood neighborhood on Fordham Road and the Grand Concourse. Knowing that he was about to be arrested, Molinas had one last trick up his sleeve. On the bugged phones he casually explained to Hacken that a certain team was an absolute lock in a game to be played a few days thence in Philadelphia.

The eavesdropping cops and detectives were overjoyed. Many of them borrowed huge amounts of money to bet on what was certainly a sure thing. Many others took out second mortgages to follow suit. And they all raced down to Philadelphia to witness the game that would make them rich beyond their dreams. But the "tip" was a hoax. Of course, Molinas attended the same game, just to laugh at the chumps who had gone broke thinking they had outconned the king of con men.

Molinas was arrested two days later. Found guilty, he was sentenced to fifteen years on a bribery and conspiracy charge that normally would have resulted in a two-year sentence.

However, Molinas's term in Attica did nothing to end his gambling addiction. He used homing pigeons to arrange and collect bets, winning a bundle on the Cassius Clay–Sonny Liston bout. Moreover, once or twice every week, Molinas was accompanied by a pair of detectives and allowed to spend several hours on the loose in order to place "inside" bets on basketball games for a certain federal judge. Molinas also used his free time to study, make judicious investments, and earned a small fortune in the stock market.

Molinas also gave free advice to any prisoner who asked and freely distributed some of the choice food he was able to purchase from guards and cooks he bribed. However, even though he was routinely promised a reduced sentence and an early parole if he gave up the names of the Mafia chieftains who had bankrolled him, Molinas demurred.

In any event, mostly thanks to the now wealthy federal judge, Molinas's sentence was reduced to seven and a half years. After serving a few days more than fifty months, Molinas was paroled on July 2, 1968.

Shortly thereafter, he applied for and received permission to move to Los Angeles. Once there Molinas got involved in several projects. One consisted of his financing and appearing at least once in soft-porn movies. Since a Mob-run laboratory was the only site where such films could be processed, Molinas reconnected with some characters who were more unsavory than he was.

In addition, Molinas frequently neglected to pay the processing bills. He figured that the bills were padded anyway, and as long as he never lied or made false promises to pay, his zipped lips in Attica would keep him safe. In fact, the Mob was so appreciative that he hadn't ratted on them, they invited Molinas to come to Las Vegas and gamble with the house's money. It was an invitation that Molinas accepted eagerly and often. As it turned out, too often. He also made several unsuccessful attempts to sell his life story to the major film studios.

Molinas did succeed in finding several highly competitive ball games at several playgrounds in the area. Among the other players were such esteemed NBA veterans as Jerry West, Rudy LaRusso, Jim McMillian, Elgin Baylor, and Wilt Chamberlain. Molinas not only held his own, but often instructed them on the proper way to set picks, make timely cuts, and throw accurate passes.

Just to keep his hand in the game, Molinas booked small-stakes bets. He also continued to bet on every basketball and football game that caught his interest. Plus, as with all his other ventures, his stock market investments were paying significant dividends.

And Molinas knew how to live the good life. He smoked

expensive Cuban cigars, ate in posh restaurants, drove a top-of-the-line Mercedes-Benz, and occasionally bedded a movie star. The fact that he continued to gamble away huge chunks of money during his frequent trips to Las Vegas never bothered him. Especially since he never moved to settle his debts there. *Hey, weren't the dagos who ran the casinos still giving him a pass for not snitching on them?*

Next up was buying and selling second mortgages on residential properties—a deal that earned Molinas seven hundred Gs in two years. He also provided the financial backing that enabled a friend to open a record store. Then Molinas got involved with a company that manufactured rockets attached to balloons that were marketed as survival devices to hikers. The money poured in, and he spent it just as quickly. Molinas knew that he was still gold.

Then Molinas got himself into real trouble. A representative of the Mob hooked Molinas up with Bernie Gusoff, who was Brooklyn born and bred and had a successful past in the fur business back in New York. But Gusoff's business was on the verge of collapse after he moved to Los Angeles.

This was a perfect setup for the Mob. They supplied the cash that set up Molinas and Gusoff in "Berjac," which was ostensibly a legitimate business that sold fur coats and leather garments. However, the real reason Berjac existed was to provide an outlet for the local Mafia to sell stolen furs.

But Gusoff was a poor businessman and bought more furs than he could move. With a refrigerated warehouse stuffed with furs, Berjac had to discount its goods just to pay expenses. The situation was so dire that Molinas was moved to apply to a Mafia moneyman for a loan. His request for $247,000 was granted with one condition—both Molinas and Gusoff were required to take out $250,000 life insurance policies on each other's lives. Each partner was the beneficiary of both policies, with the understanding that the money would then be given to the Mob.

The trouble started when Berjac failed to make the required payments on the loan. But if Gusoff neglected to pay the premiums on

Molinas's policy, which soon lapsed, Molinas never missed a payment on his partner's life insurance.

When Gusoff was mysteriously beaten to death, Molinas collected the $250,000. Did Molinas have his partner killed? Or did the Mob merely send a message to Molinas to find a way to start paying his debts to them? Whatever the truth, Molinas kept the $250,000 and celebrated by paying $54,000 for a Rolls-Royce convertible.

Then on a Saturday evening in August 1972, while Molinas was admiring the view from the patio of his new home in the Los Angeles hills, a professional assassin sneaked up behind him and fired a shot into the back of his neck, and Jack Molinas was dead.

In the end, Molinas certainly had the basketball talent to be a bona fide Hall of Famer. But his hubris was so great that he measured success in terms that he could never totally achieve. He was ambitious. He was amoral. But when we take off our faces at midnight, Jack Molinas is, in some ways, who we really want to be, who we are afraid to be. And, maybe, in our worst nightmares, Jack Molinas is who we fear we really are.

Testimony: Neal Walk

If Neal Walk ranks behind only Dolph Schayes and Rudy LaRusso as the best Jewish player in the history of the NBA, his life and times were certainly the most interesting, as well as the most tragic, of any of his coreligionists who played at that level. Here's more of his story.

His father moved the family to Cleveland in 1954 and five years later to Miami. After having a "normal Jewish, middle-class childhood," Walk eventually enrolled in Miami Beach High School. "A lot of the students drove to school in Corvettes and Rolls-Royces, but I took the bus. Because I had skipped a grade in transferring from Cleveland, I was two years younger than my classmates. I was also six nine, a hundred and eighty pounds, and looked like a concentration camp survivor. I made the varsity as a junior because I could shoot, but I had no strength and no endurance. And, even though I was an athlete, I was socially invisible." Neal calls his high school coach "a prick" who made his players run a hundred laps carrying sandbags. "He was a cracker from West Virginia not comfortable coaching so many Jews."

As a result of his averaging fifteen points and nine rebounds as a senior, Walk accepted a full ride to the University of Florida. "When I got to Gainesville, I was in a constant daze as a freshman and frustrated because freshmen were not allowed to play varsity ball. Things weren't much better in my first varsity season because I got pushed around by guys who were bigger, stronger, and were as much as five years older than me."

After his sophomore year, Walk spent a lot of time in the weight room and tipped the scales at 255. But his knees ached so much that he was booed out of a Four Tops concert because he had to stand to ease the pain.

In his initial four starts as a junior, Walk averaged thirty points and twenty rebounds—but then defenses began zeroing in on him. Still, despite being double- and triple-teamed in his senior season, Walk averaged twenty-four and seventeen and was named a first-team All-American. "Even though Gainesville was the drug capital of the world, I focused entirely on hoops. When forced to introduce myself at a fraternity mixer, I identified myself as a basketball player."

Phoenix and Milwaukee had finished the 1968–69 season tied for the worst record in the NBA, so a coin flip decided which team would get the first draft pick. The Bucks won and selected Lew Alcindor. Neal Walk was then tabbed by the Suns and thereafter deemed to be Phoenix's booby prize. "I never paid attention to that bullshit. How many guys would love to be the second overall pick?"

Walk subsequently signed a three-year contract worth a total of $825,000. "I spent a lot of money on clothes. I was dap. Custom-made suits, monogrammed shirts. Later I saw that it was all a sham and dumped my entire wardrobe."

During the preseason he accidentally crossed paths with Wilt Chamberlain. "The Dip got me laid, and I also followed Jerry West around and fucked lots of his rejects."

Walk got "his ass kicked" by the likes of Elvin Hayes, Willis Reed, and Walt Bellamy ("the dirtiest player of all time, who'd trip you, slap your face, and gouge your eyes"). If Bells was the dirtiest, Jim "Crazy Horse" Barnett was the looniest. Once when Neal shared a joint with Barnett, Crazy Horse went nuts. "He accused me of wanting to fuck him."

Walk lived the high life, sleeping with movie stars and partying with the jet set, so he wasn't at all upset when, during the Maurice Stokes charity game in the Catskills, a trio of future Hall of Famers "stole my weed."

Walk was in the middle of a drug scandal that implicated nearly the entire Suns squad in 1973. It was a story that the NBA was quick to marginalize after one of the Suns involved, Johnny High, was believed to have been killed by the Mafia-based drug dealer—and no charges were ever filed. "A minimum of 50 percent of NBA players were heavily into coke, including several who are now in the Hall of Fame. Guys on both teams would party after games. It was beautiful."

Walk's impertinent take on several of his notable contemporaries:

Walt Chamberlain—"The great unwashed."
Red Auerbach—"A pompous putz."
Elgin Baylor—"The king of prickdom."
George Gervin—"Addicted to white women and white drugs."
Calvin Murphy—"At five nine, the one guy nobody wanted to mess with."
Jerry West—"A total lunatic."
Elvin Hayes—"Called the saintly Tex Winter the 'anti-Christ' for asking him to set picks and pass."

During one game that he'll never forget, Walk boxed Dale Schlueter off the boards and was rewarded with a forearm chop to the base of his neck that put him out of action for several days. "That cheap-shot motherfucker had no NBA skills. Like too many other guys in the league, he was nothing more than a thug. I also think that the injury to my neck might have caused all that happened later."

Walk also got married in Phoenix. "I bought the whole blueprint.

Get married at twenty-four, have kids at twenty-six. Like Zorba said, 'The whole catastrophe.' Still, I broke the convention by marrying a biker chick who already had two boys by two different fathers. We were finis after nine months."

During the 1971–72 NBA season, the six-foot-ten Neal Walk stood tall among his peers, averaging 20.2 points and 12.4 rebounds per game for the Suns. By 1973 Walk started to "evolve"—he became a vegetarian; grew a beard; wore only jeans, sneakers, and sweats; and lost twenty-five pounds. Instead of being a dreadnought scorer in the low post, Walk became a finesse player who depended on his outside shooting and passing. He also studied kung fu, had a yoga practice, and began to think that he was more than just a basketball player. Hey, he'd just averaged 20 and 12, right? That was good enough for him. He didn't need to be an All-Star to satisfy his hoops ego. "The Suns were not happy about their center eating sprouts instead of eating furniture. Besides, I was told that management didn't like my friends. So I got traded to New Orleans."

His new coach, Scotty Robertson, thought Walk was "a head case." During one practice session Walk was shooting free throws when Robertson said, "What are you thinking about?"

"I want to be one with the rim."

Robertson walked away cursing.

But Walk had a great connection with the team's most celebrated player, Pete Maravich. "Pete's father made him nuts. Pete used to talk about being ready when the alien spaceships came for him."

Robertson was replaced by Butch van Breda Kolff, "a narrow-minded drunk." Like his predecessor, VBK believed Walk was crazy. "I loved to provoke him, especially when we were waiting in an airport for our flight to depart. I'd sit on the floor in a lotus position eating something with chopsticks, and Butch would shake his head, then go to the bar and have another drink. I also started smoking pot before practice."

The end of his sojourn in New Orleans came when Walk defended a high pick-and-roll by switching on to the shooter and his guard failed to switch—leaving the unattended big man to grab the missed shot and execute a resounding dunk. VBK yanked Walk from the game, saying, "Fuck you. Go sit at the end of the bench."

"Okay," said Neal. "And fuck you, too."

Walk didn't get off the bench for the next few games.

It was no surprise when VBK approached Walk before a practice. "The hardest part of being a coach is trading players," van Breda Kolff began.

"Cut the shit," said Neal. "Where and who for?"

"Fuck you, Walk. Get the fuck out of here."

Traded to the Knicks, Walk dug Red Holzman right away. "He opened the door of his hotel room dressed only in boxer shorts and white socks and smoking a big cigar. 'Glad to have you,' he said. 'Phil Jackson endorsed you. Anyway, go see Dick Barnett, and he'll show you the plays. All I care about is defense."

Here was Holzman's standard pregame speech: "Go the fuck out there and do what you know how to do."

Anybody on the court could raise his hand and call the next offensive play: "And we all respected one another's judgment. We always went with the hot hand or to the guy who was being guarded by a fish." During most time-outs, Holzman would say, "You guys do the offense. Leave me out of it."

Everybody paid rapt attention whenever Dave DeBusschere, Walt Frazier, Dick Barnett, or Phil Jackson made a suggestion in the team's huddle.

Walk loved playing with the Knicks. "It was the Great Spirit rewarding me for everything I'd ever done in my life."

In New York Neal lived about a mile from Madison Square Garden and developed the habit of getting high walking to home games. "It helped me focus and get locked in to the game. But sometimes I'd stop playing and just watch the action. I'd say to the guy who'd just beaten me, 'Hey, man, that was a hell of a nice move.' Looking back, getting stoned before games was not a great idea."

Phil Jackson lived only two blocks away and tried to get Walk to forego getting high. "During the summer Phil drove me out to his homestead in Montana in his van and worked on me all the way. But I loved the idea of being a hippie hooper. PJ did, however, succeed in getting me interested in Native American culture."

The end of his NBA career was nigh when the Knicks were purchased by Gulf and Western and management made several bad moves. "First they tried to lure Chamberlain out of retirement, which made all of the bigs on the team feel we were disposable. Then they brought in Spencer Haywood, a.k.a. Spencer Deadwood. This guy had no idea how to play. He'd bitch at the refs instead of getting back on defense, couldn't set picks, and only wanted to shoot."

Shortly thereafter, Holzman took Walk aside to say, "The shittiest part of being a coach . . ."

"I understand," said Neal.

Walk then moved in with "a crazy chick, her crazy kids, and her crazy mother" in a renovated barn in rural Connecticut. "I spent the rest of the winter snorting coke, smoking pot, reading, and playing with my dog Righteous."

When his agent relayed an offer to either finish the season with the Detroit Pistons or play in Italy, Walk let Righteous make the decision. "When I proposed going to Detroit, Righteous didn't move. When I asked him about Italy, he started barking."

The competition in Italy was rugged. "But playing in various tournaments against the Yugos was like being in a wrestling match. If you tried to box them off the boards, they'd just smash you to the floor. They made Bellamy seem like somebody's old-maid auntie."

Walk was in Italy for only a few months before he was busted for possession of "some delicious black hash"—and spent three days in jail. "Blood and shit on the walls. A thin stained mattress. The only window boarded up. There was nothing I could do but get through it all."

Since he was caught with twenty grams of the stuff, he was liable to be sent away for a few years. But when he was momentarily ignored during questioning, Walk reached out, tore off a big chunk of the hash, and ate it. With the stash now reduced to only sixteen grams, Walk was subjected to only a stiff fine and released. "I did get a nice little buzz out of the experience."

Despite playing for another know-nothing coach, Walk averaged twenty and ten. But because the team had not won the championship, new American players were sought and Walk was cut.

In the summer of 1980 Neal wandered around Saint Eustatius, a Dutch island in the Caribbean, for three days, neither eating nor drinking. He was on a vision quest, a search for spiritual guidance and purpose, "the truth of my soul." He saluted the four directions of the earth and awaited a sign. Finally, the ocean whispered, "Joshua." Overhead he saw a pair of hawks circling. Shortly thereafter, he legally changed his name to Joshua Hawk. "This was a way to release myself from my singular identification with basketball. I separated me from *me*."

After that playing in Israel was a mixed blessing. Walk liked the climate, the food, the willing women, and the chance to travel through the country. He also liked being with "my own people," admiring their courage, resourcefulness, and general cheerfulness.

However, the competition was "shitty." To keep himself "amused," he shot only bank jumpers and wrong-handed (righty) hooks and passed the ball every chance he got. He played in Israel for three seasons—"one season too long."

Back in the States he devoted a summer to lifting, running, and eating meat in response to an invitation to the training camp of the LA Clippers. "All the balls bouncing gave me a headache. The drills were boring. I was thirty-three and no longer had the burn, so I quit. My time as a professional hooper was officially over. Actually, I was relieved. Now I could get on with my real life."

Since he never cared much for money, he was practically broke. He failed broadcasting auditions, sold cosmetics out of a kiosk in a mall for five dollars an hour, dated a porn star, wrote poetry, snorted coke, rode his bicycle, was a drywaller, and worked for ten months assisting a chiropractor friend. But his left knee was aching, his right knee was constantly hyperextending, and he had to walk staircases backward to ease his pain.

In 1985 Walk was invited to attend a reunion game in Phoenix. Even though he was unable to play, he dug being back there and decided to move to Phoenix. Then his legs got worse. "My right buttock had an uncontrollable perpetual twitch. And when I stood up, I had to grab onto something until my legs stopped twitching."

Several spinal taps and MRIs discovered a knuckle-sized lump in the T-3/4 area. He might have had it from birth or from some athletic trauma ("Fucking Dale Schlueter!"); the doctors didn't know. But they agreed that his condition could eventually get worse, cutting his spinal cord and leaving him crippled. However, there was a 60 percent chance that the tumor was either on the cord or wrapped around it—in which case it could be lasered off with no real damage done. Unfortunately, the tumor was inside the cord, and Walk's legs were paralyzed. His only consolation was that his bladder and bowels were functional. "Plus, my dick was still alive."

Walk worked like a demon in rehab, pausing only when his friends moved him up to the roof to smoke a joint or two or three. "At first, I was hopeful that I would walk again. But I had trouble transferring myself from my bed to my wheelchair so I could use the toilet. One time I fell to the floor, and when the nurses were slow to come, I shit all over myself. That's when it finally hit me. I broke down and cried for about a half hour. I wanted my mom to come and save me." After two and a half years, the rehab gained nothing.

The Phoenix Suns provided him with a hand-controlled Volvo and gave him a job in the community relations department, making inspirational speeches to other handicapped folks.

The only other time I broke down and cried was when I was supposed to deliver an inspirational talk to some kids with cerebral palsy. Their bodies were all locked up, their faces clenched, and they were practically speechless. I apologized and excused myself, saying I'd come back at a later date. Which I never did.

I'd get stuck in small bathrooms, my wheelchair would sometimes escape my grasp and roll away, and I once fell out of my chair and broke a leg. But at first, I didn't want people to help me. I was surly. I could do that shit myself. Then I realized that people wanted to help me out. It made them feel good.

Still, his life was fraught with gloomy times. "I had to beat myself up to get out of my funks. 'You piece of shit! Do you want to dry up and blow away? Or learn to live with this?' There was really no choice."

Walk then took up wheelchair basketball. "It was highly competitive, even vicious. Guys would flip you whenever they could, and you had to tuck your head when you went down to protect yourself. When opponents got too physical, I'd just elbow them in the throat and they'd back off." Walk's advantages here were his long arms and ability to palm the ball. He had fifteen-foot range, and his long-armed lefty shots were never blocked. Also, "Guys simply didn't know how to play. How to deal with picks. How to box out. I was one of the slower players, but I could own the boards when I got into the attack zone. There was one game in Tucson when a fourteen-year-old girl shadowed me in the backcourt and wouldn't let me cross the time line. I tried spinning and rolling, but she was too quick and I couldn't get past her. I got so frustrated that I finally just grabbed the rail of her chair and flipped her over." Walk played on very good teams for five years, "but it beat the shit out of my hands, so I had to quit."

In March 1990 Walk was named the Wheelchair Athlete of the Year and presented a plaque by George H. W. Bush during a ceremony in the White House. "It was a bullshit honor. There were plenty of wheelchair hoopers who were much better than me, but since I was a well-known NBA veteran, giving me the award generated an inordinate amount of publicity." At the awards ceremony several "goddesses of the silver screen who I had fucked out of their socks made believe they didn't know me, even after I made sure to reintroduce myself."

In 2000 Walk swallowed his pride and started using a power chair. "That's because my hands and wrists were constantly swollen, but the battery weighs four hundred pounds, so getting stuck or running out of juice is a serious problem. Still, I haven't fallen in years."

During his speeches Walk reiterated Marine Corps slogans: "Improvise, overcome, and adapt." "Being handicapped does not mean you can't have a meaningful life."

He was fired by the Suns in 2014 for no discernible reason. "All I could figure was the penny-pinching and probable anti-Semitism of the team's new owner. I knew I might be in trouble a month before when I was interviewed by a human resources representative. 'What are your long-term goals?' I was asked. 'To make it home safely and have sex with my new wife.'"

Until his death in the summer of 2015, he survived mostly on his NBA pension and by drinking tequila to soothe the painful spasms in his legs. He also received Botox injections in his atrophied calves, quads, and thighs. "I'm just trying to be mindful," he said, "engaged in the present. To be able to listen while the universe speaks. Sometimes it speaks in whispers. Sometimes in sonic booms. Once I came to terms with living in my chair, I can listen better than I ever could before."

21

....

The Jewish Olympics

During the summer of 1912 the Fifth Olympic Games were held in Stockholm, the capital city of Sweden. More than two thousand athletes from twenty-four countries participated in several traditional competitions, including swimming and diving, soccer, shooting, rowing, cycling, tennis, various equestrian events, wrestling, plus the decathlon and pentathlon (which were both won by Jim Thorpe). In addition, solid-gold medals were awarded in a tug-of-war as well as such arts as painting, sculpture, music composition, and literature. There were also several "demonstration sports," whose adherents hoped would be included in forthcoming Olympic competition. These included baseball and *park*, a form of tennis with seven players on each side.

Yosef Yekutieli was a Russian-born fifteen-year-old, then living in Eretz Yisroel, who was energized by the newspaper reports of the grand event. He was so energized that he conceived the fanciful notion of a similar international competition for Jewish athletes to be held in Palestine.

Yekutieli spent several years developing the necessary details for his proposal to become a viable reality. Possible venues, specific competitions, promotional ideas, and potential sponsors were on his list when, in 1928, he presented his plan to the Jewish National Fund. His notion was that what he called the Maccabiada would be held to commemorate the eighteen hundredth anniversary of the Bar Kochba (the Jewish revolt against the Romans). His proposal quickly gained the support of the Eretz Israel Soccer Association as well as other sports groups in the Holy Land. Then, in the fall of 1931, Sir Arthur Wauchope, the high commissioner of British Palestine, likewise endorsed the idea.

Accordingly, the first Maccabiah (as they were now called) opened on March 28, 1932, in Tel Aviv. Approximately 400 athletes from eighteen nations competed in competitions ranging from soccer to swimming, from handball to track and field. There were sixty-nine athletes from Syria and Egypt, while the U.S. delegation of ten participants was the smallest. The leading medal-winning countries were Poland and Austria, with the United States finishing third.

The games were such a rousing success that Maccabiah II took place only three years later, with 1,350 participants representing twenty-eight countries. Because there were strict restrictions on Jewish immigration at the time, many athletes seized the opportunity to remain in Palestine. These included several members of the German contingent plus the entire Bulgarian team.

Maccabiah III was originally scheduled to convene in 1938, but was canceled due to the rise of the Nazis and increased Arab violence in Palestine. The games resumed in 1950, with 800 athletes from nineteen countries competing in the independent state of Israel.

Basketball was first introduced as a medal sport in 1950. This was before the college betting scandal broke, so three fixers from CCNY—Ed Roman, Al Roth, and Herb Cohen—represented the United States. This was a dynamic squad that easily beat Israel for the gold medal. Indeed, except for the 1957 games—when Canada beat Great Britain in the gold-medal game—the United States and Israel faced off in every championship contest.

Maccabiah IV convened in 1953. From that time until the present, the Jewish Olympics were held every four years. In 1962 the Latin American Maccabiah Games were initiated in Buenos Aires, Brazil. Ranking behind only the Olympic Games and the Pan-American

Games, the Israeli Maccabiah Games is the third-largest international sporting event in the world. By Maccabiah XVII in 2005, 6,667 athletes from fifty-four countries were on hand. Nowadays, the Maccabiah competition is organized into four distinct divisions—Juniors, Open, Masters, and Disabled.

Some notable American participants in basketball have been Larry Brown, Art Heyman, Danny Schayes (Dolph's son), and Ernie Grunfeld.

I, for one, can personally relate to the unofficial motto of the Maccabiah Games: "Two weeks to experience and a lifetime to remember."

Testimony: Maccabiah VI

As a junior I'd averaged twenty-four points and sixteen rebounds a game for Hunter College during the 1960–61 season. As a result, some committee selected me to become a member of the U.S. team at Maccabiah VI to be held in Tel Aviv in August 1961.

Years later highly competitive tryouts were held to determine the roster, but back then there were different criteria: Big-time players like Art Heyman (Duke), Larry Brown (North Carolina), Art Kaminsky (Yale), Mike Cingiser (Brown), Julie Cohen (Miami), and Sandy Pomerantz (Washington–St. Louis) were shoo-ins, with all expenses paid. I presume that, like me, the rest of the players were added to the squad only if and when they managed to raise a sum that I remember as being about three hundred dollars. Again, according to my recollections, Hunter College came up with my share.

We all met for the first time while boarding the bus that would take us to Kutsher's for a seven-day training session. Heyman quickly established himself as the team's tummler—laughing, joking, conducting himself as though he knew he was the best player on the team. Even Larry Brown laughed at Heyman's tomfoolery, which was a distinct surprise.

During his sophomore season Heyman starred for the varsity team, and as usual North Carolina and Duke continued their bitter intrastate rivalry. On February 4, 1961, the Duke and North Carolina freshman teams had played the first game of the doubleheader. There were multiple fights during that game, and North Carolina had finished the game with only three players on the floor (five North Carolina players had fouled out, and three more had been ejected for fighting). Early in the subsequent varsity game, Heyman was involved in two incidents, where he first pushed over a fan who he thought was attacking him and then in the closing minutes of the game, while trying to protect a slim Duke lead, committed a hard foul against UNC's point guard Larry Brown, who was attempting to drive to the hoop. Brown threw the ball and then a punch at Heyman, touching off a general melee that saw future basketball executive Donnie Walsh, then a substitute player for North Carolina, also attack Heyman. The melee lasted about ten minutes, and despite Heyman being ejected for fighting, his thirty-six points had given Duke the victory, 81–77. Brown, Walsh, and Heyman were all suspended for the remainder of the ACC season.

On the bus Heyman took a folded newspaper article from his wallet and proudly passed it around to his new teammates. The article was a report of the now infamous tussle. Brown refused to read it and simply passed it on.

When we finally arrived at Kutsher's, we all headed straight for the outdoor basketball court. All of us were wearing sneakers, so it seemed entirely natural to begin playing three-on-three half-court games.

I was teamed up with Heyman and Brown. Growing up in the Bronx, I certainly knew how to play in this abbreviated game. Making timely passes and hitting midrange jumpers, I played well. Still, Heyman was the dominant force as we won our first two games. Then Pomerantz and his sidekicks took the court against us.

Pomerantz was a slender, tensile-strong six foot five who had been an All-American at University City High School in St. Louis before accepting a scholarship to the University of Cincinnati. However, because of several anti-Semitic incidents, he'd transferred to Washington University (WU) in St. Louis, which would be his destination in the fall.

And Pomerantz proceeded to use and abuse Heyman—hitting jumpers, driving for layups, even blocking shots. Heyman reacted first with disbelief and then with mounting anger. He called a shooting foul on Pomerantz when it was clear that no contact had occurred. Then Heyman seemed to flip when Pomerantz stole his dribble.

Heyman's retaliation was shameful. The next time Pomerantz went up to launch his jumper, Heyman crouched and threw a shoulder into his opponent's knees. To me, and judging by the raised eyebrows among the rest of the guys, there was no doubt that Heyman's act was deliberate. For the next few days, Heyman took it upon himself to cheerfully steer Pomerantz's wheelchair all around the resort. And, of course, Pomerantz, left early and missed the trip. However, the injury turned out to be just a severe sprain, and Pomerantz's recovery was sufficient for him to earn Small-College All-American honors at WU.

Once practice started under the direction of Donald "Dudey" Moore, the coach at Duquesne, I realized in a hurry that I was way out of my league. At Hunter we played a one-three-one zone, so I had no idea how to play man-to-man defense. On offense I played the pivot against straight-up defenses and a wing against zones. Passing? That's what my teammates did to get me the ball. Shooting? That's what I did every time I touched the ball. Setting picks? Who, me?

So when Moore instituted a high-post offense, I felt like the hoop was fifty feet behind me. No wonder I was quickly made an alternate. Still, I was presented with a gold-plated medal after the United States handily defeated Israel.

Even though I never played, my Maccabiah adventures were still lively. In fact, they were much too lively.

The entire U.S. team was one of the first to enter the Ramat Gan Stadium, which meant we had to stand in formation for several hours while the other teams made their appearances. Of course, it was hot—more than one hundred degrees—and we were wearing our official long pants, neckties, shirts, and tiny hats. Meanwhile, several little kids scooted around us, selling frosty bottles of some red liquid that they claimed were cherry sodas. And, more the fool me, I was the only one to buy me a bottle of what turned out to be red sugar water. Moreover, there must have been some additional ingredients, because I soon came down with a rousing case of diarrhea. Over the course of my "two weeks," I lost twenty-one pounds.

To make my trip either better or worse, I hooked up with a member of the U.S. swimming team, and we got married two years later. Two years after that, however, we got divorced.

So, yes, my two-week experience left me with a lifetime to remember.

22

....

Some More Blue-Chip Jewish Hoopers

If the number of influential Jewish players peaked in the late 1940s, it's quite evident that the influence went into a dramatic decline after the betting scandals of the early 1950s. Even so, there were several outstanding Jews in action dating from the 1951 Big Fix (or immediately before) to the Molinas-powered point-shaving scandal eleven years later.

In addition to those already mentioned—Rosenbluth, Dolph Schayes, Moe Becker, et al.—here are some brief sketches of several more blue-chip players of that era. The criteria are either some kind of All-American status or having played a total of twenty-five games or more in the BAA/NBA.

Irv Bemoras: All-American (1953) at Villanova; subsequently played 131 games with Milwaukee and St. Louis.

A few years back I interviewed Bemoras for a book I was writing, *The Wizard of Odds: How Jack Molinas Almost Destroyed the Game of Basketball*. Bemoras had played against Molinas several times, once in the 1953 NCAA Tournament when Illinois beat Columbia and many times in the NBA.

"Jackie was really good," Bemoras said.

"How good?"

"If he had been serious about his game and played it straight, Jackie would have been a shoo-in for the Hall of Fame."

Harry "Big Hesh" Boycoff: All-American (1943) at St. John's; in 1947 scored 54 points in one game, outscoring St. John's opponent, St. Francis (Brooklyn). Averaged 10.2 ppg (1947–51) for Toledo and Waterloo (NBL) and Boston and Tri-Cities (NBA). With the Celtics his salary of fifteen thousand dollars was the highest in the league.

Howard Carl: DePaul; Chicago (1961–62).

Phil Farbman: CCNY; Philadelphia, Boston (1948–49).

Jerry Fleishman: NYU; played with Philadelphia and New York (1946–50, 1952–53). Was a key substitute when Philadelphia won the BAA Championship in 1947.

I was fourteen years old, a big, gangly, clumsy kid who would much rather have grown up to be Joe DiMaggio than George Mikan. Anyway, I was spending my summer working in a produce store and living with my mom (who came out on weekends) in a small rental room in Rockaway. One afternoon I was casually shooting hoops at one of the baskets set up on a court on Fiftieth Street, using a bloated, bald basketball that someone had given me.

All of a sudden, some guy appeared on the court, dribbling a brand-new ball. He stood a bit over six feet tall, was perhaps a solid 180 pounds, and looked to be in terrific shape.

"Do you mind?" he said, nodding toward the basket I was using.

"Not at all."

"Let's use this ball, okay?"

We would up playing one-on-one, and he totally thrashed me with power drives and long two-handed set shots.

Afterward, he asked if I wouldn't mind his showing me a few "pointers."

So I learned the proper way to shoot layups, how to dribble and shoot with my left hand, as well as how to make various passes.

We didn't make a formal introduction until we were done.

"Charley Rosen," I said.

"Pleased to meet you, Charley. Stick with it. With your size and coordination you have a chance to become a pretty good player. . . . Oh, my name is Jerry Fleishman."

Wow! Of course I knew who he was. And from that moment on, both he and Mikan were my heroes.

Donnie Forman: NYU; Minneapolis (1948–49).

Larry Friend: California; 1957–58 Knicks.

Leo Gottlieb: no college; New York (1946–48).

Rollen Hans: LIU; Baltimore Bullets (1953–55).

Sidney "Sonny" Hertzberg: CCNY; New York, Washington, Boston (1946–51). Led the Celtics in scoring with 10.2 ppg in 1949–50 season.

William "Red" Holzman: CCNY; Rochester (1946–54). He was a member of Rochester's NBA champs in 1951 and a two-time All-Star as well.

Louis Herman "Red" Klotz: Villanova; played in only eleven games with Baltimore (1947–48), but was best known for playing with, coaching, and owning the perennial patsies who lost to the Harlem Globetrotters. His teams had various names, among them the Washington Generals (after Klotz's hero, Dwight Eisenhower), the New York Nationals, the New Jersey Reds, the World All-Stars, and the Boston Shamrocks. Klotz played until he was sixty and was still playing half-court pickup games into his eighties.

Klotz first encountered the Globetrotters in 1949 when he was playing for the Spas. After the Spas beat the Globetrotters twice in two weeks, Abe Saperstein, the touring team's founder and owner, asked Klotz to form a team that would travel with the Globetrotters and play them night after night. As such Klotz's outfits won two games in more than fourteen thousand played—with one victory coming when he hit a set shot at the final buzzer. The other came when the scoreboard operator missed a couple of points scored by the underdogs, but the score book proved that they had won.

"Beating the Globetrotters," he said, "is like shooting Santa Claus."

Lionel Malamed: CCNY; Indianapolis, Rochester (1948-49).

Saul Mariaschin: Harvard; Boston (1947-48).

Carl Meinhold: LIU; Baltimore Bullets, Chicago Stags, Providence Steamrollers (1947-49).

Nat Militzok: CCNY; New York, Toronto (1946-47).

Ed Miller: Syracuse; averaged 10.2 ppg with Milwaukee and Baltimore (1952-54).

Howie Rader: LIU; Tri-Cities in the NBL and Baltimore in the NBA (1946-49).

Arnie Risen: Ohio State; was a four-time All-Star while playing for Rochester (1948-55), Boston (1955-58).

Alexander "Petey" Rosenberg: St. Joseph's; member of Philadelphia's championship team (1947).

Hank Rosenstein: CCNY; New York, Providence (1947).

Irv Rothenberg: LIU; Cleveland, Washington, St. Louis, New York (1946-49).

Mickey Rottner: Loyola of Chicago; Sheboygan (NBL) and Chicago (1945–48).

Marv Schatzman: Born a Jew but converted to Catholicism at Syracuse; played thirty-four games for Baltimore (1949–50).

Art Spector: Villanova; Boston (1946–50).

Sid Tannenbaum: NYU; New York, Baltimore (1948–49).

Irv Torgoff: LIU; Washington, Baltimore, Philadelphia (1946–49).

>   According to Red Auerbach, "Torgoff was really the first player who became known as a sixth man in basketball. He was the kind of player who could come off the bench and was as good as any of the starters. He could turn a whole game around. He was one of the great players."

Max Zaslofsky: St. John's; ranks second only to Dolph Schayes as the best Jewish player of this time period. With Chicago, New York, Baltimore, Milwaukee, and Fort Wayne (1946–56) averaged 14.8 ppg with highs of 21.0 (1947–48) and 20.6 (1948–49) with Chicago. Was twice an All-Star and in 1947 was named to the All-NBA team as a rookie.

In addition to those Jewish players who had some success in the BAA/NBA, three were named to various All-American teams during this period.

Jeff Cohen: William and Mary (1958–61). Drafted in the second round by the Chicago Packers, Cohen signed instead with the Hawaii Chiefs in the ABL. He then played with the Chicago Motor until the league folded in the spring of 1962.

Donald Goldstein: Louisville (1957–59). He was a member of the gold-medal U.S. team at the 1959 Pan-American Games, where his most notable teammates were Oscar Robertson and Jerry West. Although Goldstein was drafted in the second round (tenth overall) by the Detroit Pistons, he opted for dental school.

Alan Seiden: St. John's (1957–59). He was a second-round draft pick (twelfth overall) of the St. Louis Hawks, but left the team when he remained on the bench during a blowout loss in a preseason game. "Ed Macauley was the Hawks coach," Seiden said. "When I asked him why I hadn't played, he said that he forgot I was on the bench. So I went home to Brooklyn."

Seiden did continue his professional career by playing with the Pittsburgh Rens (1961–62) in the newly formed American Basketball League. (The ABL was founded by Abe Saperstein after the NBA refused to allow him to buy an expansion team that would be located on the West Coast.)

Testimony: David Stern

Maurice Podoloff retired in 1963 and was replaced by Walter Kennedy. In 1967 the title of NBA president was changed to NBA commissioner. Larry O'Brien succeeded Kennedy in 1975 and was, in turn, replaced by David Stern in 1984. Here's what Stern had to say when I interviewed him in 1996:

> I was born in the Chelsea section of Manhattan, on Nineteenth Street and Ninth Avenue, back in 1942, when a sense of neighborhood and family community was important. I grew up in an apartment house where my family lived on the third floor, my grandmother lived on the fourth floor, and one of my aunts lived on the second floor. I went through the elementary grades at PS 11, the same school that my mother and my older sister had previously attended. My father's delicatessen was on Eighth Avenue between Twenty-Second and Twenty-Third. My grandfather's butcher shop was on Eighth Avenue and Eighteenth Street. And many of my friends were the sons of local merchants.

It was always a big deal when my father got some free tickets to a baseball game from one of his beer suppliers. Ballantine sponsored the Yankees. A home run was a Ballantine Blast. Schaefer sponsored the Dodgers, and Knickerbocker beer was the Giants' sponsor. Myself, I was a diehard Giants fan. So Willie Mays was much better than Mickey and the Duke. I also liked the Giants because they had the first all-black outfield, with Mays, Hank Thompson, and Monte Irvin.

In addition to avidly rooting for the Giants, I was also a devoted Knick fan. Going uptown to Madison Square Garden on Fifty-Seventh Street was another big treat. Admission was fifty cents with a GO card. I lived to watch the NBA doubleheaders, the Syracuse Nationals against the Fort Wayne Zollner Pistons, then maybe the Knicks versus the Minneapolis Lakers. I grew up with a definite sense of sports being a good influence on people's lives. And so, totally apart from my Hebrew tradition, I read the newspapers from back to front.

I had several basketball heroes, mostly the big, slow guys like Charlie Tyra and Phil Jordan. That's probably because I'm the same size now as I was when I was eleven: five foot nine and three-quarter inches.

Of course I played basketball. On my synagogue team, then when I went to Rutgers, I played in the Teaneck Rec League. I tried to model my jump shot after Jimmy Baechtold, but I never had any pretensions of being a real player. I was a reliable defender, and if I ever did wind up with the ball, I'd pass it quickly to someone who could shoot. Even when I got my nose broken trying to rebound with the big guys, playing basketball was always fun.

Even so, baseball was always the national pastime. By the very nature of the game, baseball has all the advantages of tradition. If basketball is an appointment, baseball is a cultural ubiquity. During the course of an average baseball game, there are numerous time delays: a pitcher coming in from the bullpen or a pinch hitter coming out of the dugout, just the natural pauses between pitches.

That means lots of time for the broadcasters to reminisce, expand on any topic, and act the raconteur. Whereas basketball, hey, it's forty-eight minutes of nonstop action. We go to commercials during every time-out, but the fans want to hear about what's going on in the game at hand even during foul shots.

At the same time, we're trying to build a sense of tradition for the NBA. How old was Major League Baseball when Babe Ruth was in his heyday? Just about fifty years, right where we are now. And I will proudly take credit for the first NBA Legends Game we had at the 1984 All-Star Game. Our new video, *The NBA at 50*, is our latest attempt to present our own history to the latest generation of basketball fans. We've also sent copies of the video to every player in the league. But it's difficult to really understand something that hasn't happened in your own cognitive lifetime. Even so, more people have heard of Babe Ruth than know George Mikan, and I'm still not sure how to deal with that.

Anyway, here's how I got where I am now . . . While I was attending Columbia Law School, my first clerkship was in Stern's Delicatessen. After I graduated in 1966, I got a job at a law firm, which just happened to have the NBA as a client. Another fortunate coincidence was that the lawyer who did the NBA work was leaving to go into private practice, so I just asked for the job.

My first case was Connie Hawkins versus the NBA in 1967. The gist of the case was that Hawkins was being barred from playing in the NBA because of an alleged association with gamblers [Jack Molinas] when he was a freshman at the University of Iowa. So there I was, a rabid basketball fan getting personal testimony from some of the NBA's founders: Eddie Gottlieb, Walter Kennedy, Ben Kerner, Fred Zollner, and even Maurice Podoloff.

The NBA's official position in the Hawkins litigation was to say that whatever we were accused of doing, we didn't do. And if we did it, it was an accident. And if it was an accident, then it wasn't illegal. Even now we could still argue the merits of the case, because whatever Connie did, he was only nineteen years old. And, in fact, Commissioner Walter Kennedy had been badly misled by the New York district attorney's staff, who claimed that Hawkins was guilty of all sorts of things, but when the time came for the DA to step up, all of the promised evidence seemed to have disappeared. Anyway, at the end of the day, it was time to make a financial settlement with Connie and let him into the league.

Most of the other relevant litigations involved players' rights. We were constantly being sued by our own players, and, consequently, the NBA was still perceived by too many people as being something of an upstart organization. In fact, from 1946 until 1961, the NBA only had eight teams. To the sports world, nothing much was going on in the NBA.

I joined the NBA in 1978 as general counsel. My deal with Commissioner Larry O'Brien was for two years with a one-year option, and I fully expected to return to my firm. I wouldn't even leave the firm until they assured me that I'd be welcomed back. I've always enjoyed the practice of law because it's such a great discipline.

And then Larry asked me to get involved with broadcasting rights—cable TV and stuff like that. Then, sometime in 1981, I became executive vice president for business and legal affairs. I became commissioner when Larry retired. This was on February 1, 1984.

I inherited a good situation. In April 1983 we had averted a players' strike, and then a few months later we had finalized the antidrug agreement. Several franchises that were once on the verge of going out of business were already stabilized. Also, by the time I took office, we had just entered into a collective bargaining agreement that featured a salary cap. Instead of litigating with our players, we were negotiating with them. Most of the crises seemed to have been overcome, which reflected a lot of work that had been going on for years while Larry was commissioner. So the league was in good shape and ready to pop.

As for me, I really didn't have a master plan, but there were certain principles that guided us all. It may sound corny, but the number-one principle never changes: That the game is king. That no matter what the marketplace demanded, we never screwed around with the basic integrity of the game.

Through the years we've always been bombarded with all kinds of suggestions. The NBA should lower the basket, raise the court, make the shot clock fifty seconds. And our response was always, all right, let's study it. But, hey. Isn't it interesting how much the colleges tinker with their basic rules? First they had that five-second possession rule, which I believe is still in effect. Then it was a forty-five-second shot clock, and what is it now? Thirty seconds?

Note: Later in Stern's reign several major changes were indeed made. Instead of allowing a team ten seconds to advance the ball over the midcourt line, the allotted time was reduced to eight seconds. Modified zone defenses were allowed. And offenses were given a tremendous boost when defensive hand-checking and banging off-the-ball cutters were disallowed. No matter what reasons Stern offers, all of this was in response to the "marketplace's" demand for more scoring.

Another principle that we adhered to was the understanding that nobody was going to care about the NBA as much as we did. And so we were fiercely protective to the point of combativeness. That's why I didn't hesitate to call an executive producer and complain about the way he'd presented a certain game on TV. I'd say something like, "Your opening was a clip of a fight that happened the night before? Is that what you think the NBA is all about? I realize you've got to report on the issues, but don't profess to abhor the fight and then run it seven times so that your audience can get their jollies." So the exec would say to himself, "My God, I can't get a return call from Pete Rozelle, and here I've got the NBA commissioner calling me." And most of the time, we'd work something out.

However, our strong promotion of the "Bad Boy" Detroit Pistons was a mistake. What happened was that one of the NBA's merchandising partners came to me after Detroit's first championship and proposed that our home video for that season should be called "Bad Boys." The guy said he was behind in his video sales, and he felt strongly that the outlaw appeal would boost the marketing. Besides, everybody was already calling the Pistons "Bad Boys" anyway. So I went along with it.

And we did begin a slow process to clean up the violence that had become much too prevalent in our game. For example, we finally decided that if a player threw a single punch, whether it landed or not, he was gone. It was a matter requiring a deliberate jurisprudential analysis. The same thing with flagrant fouls. We knew something drastic had to be done after watching Kevin McHale and Kurt Rambis clotheslining each other in the 1992 playoffs.

We also eliminated hand-checking because it slowed down the game and encouraged a bump-and-grind style of play. Plus, everybody was getting annoyed. Slap that hand away, push it away, push it back. And that's not what fans were paying to see. They were watching NBA games to see great athletes doing things that no other group of athletes had ever done, or could do, before. Nobody wanted to see the players get into situations that escalated until two guys were trying to beat each other's brains in. We want to give these great athletes a chance to perform.

Now, I'm aware that there are some purists out there who are concerned that the NBA has deliberately moved the emphasis from competition to entertainment. But I totally disagree. It's always the game itself that appeals. People don't tune into Bulls games to watch the cheerleaders. And the people who watch basketball games are interested in seeing how Shaquille O'Neal impacts the Lakers. Or whether or not Larry Johnson, Allan Houston, and Chris Childs can turn the Knicks around. These are core basketball issues.

Yes, there are people who are looking for more of an entertainment experience at an NBA game. And yes, if we're going to keep growing, we'd better be attractive to television and run a lot of tune-in ads. Either we move ahead and stay with the times, or we'll fall off the charts.

It wasn't so long ago that NBC televised only five or six games on a national basis and the championship series could be seen only on tape delay. There's an old saying that's still true: Fred Astaire dances and sports leagues promote.

And look at what all our promoting has led to. In 1981 the NBA was generally considered to be drug infested, oversalaried, and too black. Okay? Now fast-forward to the 1992 Olympics, and remember how much America supported the appeal of the Dream Team. There were so many basketball heroes playing together for the first time: Larry, Magic, Michael, and a great supporting cast. It didn't matter whether you'd seen them before individually. The 1992 Olympics marked the crowning of America in its own homegrown sport.

I also like the idea of black kids in the playground shooting three-pointers and saying, "I'm Larry Bird." And white kids might be dunking and saying, "I'm Michael Jordan." That's the best of sports.

But there's also a downside. One negative perception is that NBA players are making too much money. I think this assumption raises people's expectations and makes people more critical of NBA players and pro sports in general. So I think we have to educate the sports public. Yes, these athletes are entertainers. And if you don't begrudge the money paid to Springsteen or Oprah or Madonna or Prince, then you shouldn't begrudge Michael Jordan.

But the players also have to be educated. That's part of our job and why we have rookie orientation programs. And educating the players is the union's job as well.

In sum, the NBA is a global phenomenon. Not long ago, New Jersey and Orlando played two regular-season games in Japan that drew eighty thousand fans and generated over eight million dollars. It was less the money, though, and more that we needed a game somewhere in Asia to support our three Chinese television contracts, plus our TV arrangements in Taiwan, South Korea, Hong Kong, Japan, Indonesia, Malaysia, Singapore, Australia, and the Philippines. In truth, the NBA is the most internationally popular of American sports.

With all I have to do and with everything going on, I still love attending games. But whenever I do, I have to sit there and say things like, "Isn't that interesting?" or "Hooray for the officials." So it's much more fun for me to close the door to my study, watch a ball game, and yell and scream like an everyday fan.

Who do I root for? Never mind. That's my deepest secret.

23

....

The Coaches

During the modern era there have been precious few noteworthy Jewish coaches in the college ranks. The following are a few examples.

Larry Brown at UCLA (1979–80), Kansas (1983–88), and SMU (2012–16). His teams qualified for eight NCAA Tournaments plus one NIT appearance.

Overall, Brown has had fourteen head-coaching jobs, and his first one provided a sign of things to come. On April 7, 1969, he signed on to coach at Davidson. Twelve weeks later, without having coached a game or a practice session, he left Davidson to play for the Washington Capitols in the American Basketball Association (ABA). This move began a whirlwind tour through several colleges and professional teams as Brown tried to scratch an itch that never went away.

When he coached the UCLA Bruins (1979–81), the national media considered him to be the ideal college coach—a nurturing and highly moral presence. Yet he moved on when UCLA was hit with several NCAA sanctions for illegal recruiting practices under his watch.

In 1988 Brown coached Kansas to the NCAA title. However, it was widely known that Kansas's 73–69 triumph over

Oklahoma in the championship game was aided and abetted by one of the Sooners' best players having been in league with gamblers to control the outcome. Also, within months of winning the NCAA Tournament, Brown unexpectedly quit Kansas, leaving numerous recruiting violations to be discovered in his wake. Because of Brown's illegal activities, Kansas would become the first national champion to be prevented from defending its title.

NCAA violations seemed to follow Brown as he moved from school to school. In addition to Kansas, UCLA and even SMU suffered various sanctions for irregularities in Brown's programs. Indeed, even though SMU went 25-5 in the 2015–16 season, the Mustangs were ineligible to compete in the NCAA Tournament because of a self-imposed ban for "academic improprieties and unethical conduct" in Brown's program. Moreover, the school suspended Brown for nine games for "lack of head coach control." It was widely assumed that SMU imposed these penalties on itself only because the school expected the results of an NCAA investigation would have led to more severe sanctions.

Then in July 2016, the seventy-five-year-old Brown resigned from his position at SMU because the school refused to give him a new five-year contract! There are rumors that Brown's next job will be coaching the wheelchair team at a senior housing center in Boca Raton, Florida.

Mike Cingiser was an All-American honorable mention at Brown (1960–62) and returned to his alma mater as head coach (1981–91).

Samuel Cozen at Drexel Tech (1952–69) was also Wilt Chamberlain's first coach at Overbrook High School (1950–52).

Seth Greenberg at Long Beach State (1990–96), South Florida (1996–2003), and Virginia Tech (2003–12). His teams appeared in six NIT and three NCAA Tournaments. Greenberg also coached the U.S. basketball team to a gold medal in the XIX Maccabiah Games (2013).

Harry Litwack was a veteran of the SPAHS and at Temple (1952–73) was renowned for designing new forms of zone defenses. His Owls won the NIT Championship in 1969.

Josh Paster started at Memphis (2009–16) and is now the current coach at Georgia Tech.

Dave Polansky succeeded Nat Holman at CCNY on three separate occasions (1953–54, 1957–58, 1960–71).

Jule Rivlin coached at Marshall (1957–63).

Herbert Rubenheimer was LIU's first basketball coach (1928–30).

Roy Rubin coached at LIU (1962–72).

Lou Sachs coached at Loyola of Chicago (1923–42), where he created innovative fast-break patterns and developed the two-two-one zone defense.

Red Sarachek at Yeshiva (1940–69) was instrumental in the implementation of motion offenses and trap defenses. He also mentored Red Holzman and Lou Carnesecca.

Isadore "Spin" Solario coached at Chicago Teachers College (1963–70).

Albert "Dolly" Stark coached at Dartmouth (1929–36, 1945–46).

David "Pep" Tobey was nicknamed "the coach of coaches" during his career at various New York City high schools and at Cooper Union (1947–60).

Brooklyn College has the unofficial record for employing the most Jewish basketball coaches: Pinky Match (1927–34), Venty Leib (1943–44),

Morris Raskin (1944–45, 1950–53, 1960–62), Julie Bender (1946–47), Al Kaplan (1962–67), Gary Green (1975–79), Mark Reiner (1980–90), and Ron Kestenbaum (1990–92).

In the seventy-year history of the BAA/NBA, there haven't been a large number of Jewish coaches. However, several of these men have had significant successes.

Arnold "Red" Auerbach coached the Washington Capitols (1946–49), Tri-Cities Blackhawks (1949–50), and Boston Celtics (1950–66). During his tenure on Boston's bench the team won nine championships (1957, 1959–66). Then, with Auerbach as president of the franchise, the Celtics won seven more championships (1968–69, 1974, 1976, 1981, 1984, 1986).

David Blatt coached the Cleveland Cavaliers (2014–16).

Herb Brown coached the Detroit Pistons (1975–78), but is more well known as being Larry Brown's older brother.

Phil Brownstein coached the Chicago Stags (1949–50).

Laurence Frank coached the New York Nets (2004–10) and the Detroit Pistons (2011–13).

Eddie Gottlieb coached the Philadelphia Warriors from 1946 to 1955, winning the championship in the league's inaugural season.

Lester Harrison coached the Rochester Royals (1948–55) to an NBA Championship in 1951.

Red Holzman led the Milwaukee–St. Louis Hawks (1953–57), then the Knicks (1967–77, 1978–82), winning two championships in New York (1970, 1973).

I had two contacts with Holzman, one indirect and one direct.

The first came in 1961 when he was a scout for the Knicks and I was the star player for Hunter College. We were playing

St. Francis (Brooklyn) at the 69th Regiment Armory when Holzman came to look me over as a possible draft pick. He was sitting in the first row of the bleachers located directly under our basket.

Near the end of the game, I was late getting back on defense (as was my wont), but a teammate ripped the dribble from one of the St. Francis guards and threw a long downcourt pass to me. By the time I caught the ball, I was about fifteen feet ahead of the nearest defender and headed straight for Holzman.

It should be noted that I wore a brace on my left knee to secure an annoying but seldom-painful injury I'd suffered playing schoolyard football several years before. Eventually, I'd need surgery to deal with a cartilage tear.

It should also be noted that dunking "in the face" of a defender was considered an unforgiveable insult that would lead to the dunker's getting low-bridged at some point. Dunking was permissible only in pregame layup lines or on unopposed fast breaks.

So, I had license, and was determined, to take a few hard dribbles and show Holzman how easily I could dunk the ball.

However, as I planted my left takeoff foot, my knee locked. As a result, I was only able to lift my left heel off the floorboards, slam the ball against the underside of the rim, . . . and unceremoniously crash to the floor.

Whereupon Holzman closed his notebook and made a quick exit stage right.

Needless to say, even though the draft lasted nine rounds in those days, I remained unclaimed.

Many years later Holzman was coaching the Knicks, and I had managed to hook up with *Sport Magazine* as a contributing writer. My latest assignment was to do a profile of Mike Riordan, who was a seldom-used bench player for the Knicks but became an All-Star when traded to the Baltimore Bullets.

I entered the Knicks' pregame locker room, hoping to get a quote from Holzman about why Riordan had not developed much during his three years in New York. So, holding my trusty cassette recorder in front of me like a dowsing rod, I approached Holzman and said, "Can I ask you a question about Mike Riordan?"

He looked disdainfully at my recorder and said, "I will if you put that fucking thing away."

Which I quickly did.

Even so, no matter how I framed my questions, Holzman's answer was the same.

"Why was he originally drafted only in the ninth round?"

"Mike was a good player."

"What's the difference between Riordan as a Knick and with the Bullets?"

"Mike's a good player."

"I hear your wife, Selma, makes a very good flanken."

"Mike's a good player."

Perhaps if I had indeed dunked that misbegotten shot, Holzman would at least have given me Selma's recipe.

Murray Mendenhall coached the Fort Wayne Zollner Pistons (1949–51).

Roy Rubin was positively the worst coach in NBA history. Until he was fired late in the 1972–73 season, his record in Philadelphia was 4-47. For more on Rubin's ineptitude in that horrendous, hilarious season, see my *Perfectly Awful* (University of Nebraska Press, 2014).

Dolph Schayes tried his hand at coaching the Philadelphia Warriors (1963–66), but was too nice a guy to succeed.

Dave Wohl had one season at the helm of the New Jersey Nets (1985–86).

Larry Brown's career in the professional ranks was even more controversial than his many seasons coaching college ball. Measuring only five foot nine and 160 pounds—and after a moderately successful collegiate career at North Carolina—he was deemed too slight to play in the NBA. Yet he was a three-time All-Star in the American Basketball Association (while playing for three different teams), and his twenty-three assists (February 20, 1970, Washington versus Pittsburgh) stands as the league's single-game record.

The travelogue of his subsequent professional coaching gigs begins in the American Basketball Association.

In the ABA

> Carolina Cougars (1972–74)
> Denver Nuggets (1974–76)

In the NBA

> Denver Nuggets (1976–79)
> New Jersey Nets (1981–83)
> San Antonio Spurs (1988–92)
> Los Angeles Clippers (1991–93)
> Indiana Pacers (1993–97)
> Philadelphia Sixers (1997–2003)
> Detroit Pistons (2003–5)
> New York Knicks (2005–6)
> Charlotte Hornets (2008–11)

Over the course of his long coaching career, Brown rightfully earned the reputation of being one of the best teachers of fundamental basketball in the long history of the game. Yet in the pros he made a practice of egregiously favoring players from North Carolina and the Atlantic Coast Conference over other players who had significantly better skill levels. That's precisely what happened in New Jersey when Brown's preferential treatment of Mike O'Koren (North Carolina), Mike Gminski (Duke), and a trio of Maryland products—Albert King, Len Elmore, and Buck Williams—was the despair of the Nets' non-ACC players.

With the Nets Brown devoted most of his instructional time and energy to his pets. He would also excuse them from his habitual hard-driving three-hour practices, saying that they worked so hard in games that they needed more rest than their teammates.

According to Darryl Dawkins, "'Bucko' was Larry's favorite of favorites. To keep the six-foot-eight Williams happy, Larry plugged him into the pivot and left seven-foot me out to dry on the high post. Larry had been a guard in his active days and didn't know what to do with a true center like me. So during games, I felt like I was out in the parking lot."

Brown was also from the Dean Smith school of head coaches in that he never let his assistants do much except round up loose balls. Nor would he let his assistants speak to any of the media.

While Brown was under contract with one team or another, he was also diligently seeking employment elsewhere. The circumstances of his exit from the Nets are a good example of his routine game plan.

The Nets were 47-29 and playoff bound, and Brown had unexpectedly granted his players two days off—a Sunday and a Monday. They were enjoying their minivacation but dreading the survival drill that Tuesday's practice would be.

Then Mike Weber, a reporter for the *Newark Star-Ledger*, heard a rumor that Brown was in Kansas City and about to be interviewed for the coaching job at the University of Kansas. Somehow Weber discovered the hotel and room number where Brown was supposed to be staying, so he made a phone call.

"Hello?"

"Hello? May I speak to John Williams, please?

"There's no John Williams here. This is Larry Brown."

"Hi, Larry. This is Mike Weber from the *Star-Ledger*."

BLAM! Brown hung up the phone in a hurry. But the news was out.

Turned out that the Nets' owner, Joe Taub, was incensed and fired Brown forthwith. And yes, Brown did get the Kansas job as well as an indelible nickname—"Next Town Brown."

Brown perpetually preached a "team concept." But just as

frequently, he took credit for wins and blamed his players for losses. This was particularly evident during the Athens Olympic Games in 2004. Even before the Games began, Brown was claiming that the U.S. Olympic Committee had saddled him with an inferior roster that had no chance of winning the gold. Actually, the team included such NBA luminaries as Tim Duncan, Dwyane Wade, Carmelo Anthony, Shawn Marion, and Lamar Odom, plus a pair of just-drafted players who weren't expected to see much playing time—a too young LeBron James and the underachieving Emeka Okafor. Indeed, the only players who warranted Brown's displeasure were Allen Iverson and Stephon Marbury, two chronic ball hogs and malcontents. In fact, after having coached Iverson for several seasons in Philadelphia, Brown often voiced his hatred of the diminutive guard in public interviews. (Yet once he left the City of Brotherly Love, Brown swore that AI was actually one of his all-time favorite players.) As a result of Brown's pregame criticism, his players were disheartened and were fortunate to win a bronze medal.

In 2001 Brown was clearly outcoached, as his Philadelphia Sixers were beaten in a five-game championship series by Phil Jackson's Los Angeles Lakers. Three years later Brown got his revenge when he led the Detroit Pistons to a five-game victory over the Lakers to claim the championship. However, had LA's Karl Malone not been injured early in the series, it's highly doubtful that the Pistons would have prevailed. Brown has made no secret of his detestation of Jackson, calling him "unbearably arrogant." And Jackson has returned the disfavor, calling Brown "incredibly arrogant."

Wherever he's coached he's bragged about "finally having the perfect job." Yet his average tenure with an NBA team has been only 2.7 seasons. Also, he's never left a position on good terms with any of his players or employers.

Brown has claimed that he's never been religious and has "never really believed in God." But he did become a believer during his disastrous stopover in New York: "I pray for Him to inject my guys with some intelligence and a clue. I pray, most of all, for the season to end."

Through all of his many successes and failures, Brown has usually maintained a bright, perky, and optimistic view. But perhaps he revealed the morbid bedrock of his psyche when he said this toward the end of his season in New York: "I pray sometimes for our plane to crash."

Testimony: David Blatt

On January 22, 2016, the Cleveland Cavaliers fired David Blatt, despite the fact that the team's 30-11 record was the best in the Western Conference. Blatt was mystified, saying he had no idea why he was dismissed. According to David Griffin, the Cavs' general manager, the reason had to do with "a lack of fit with our personnel and our vision." Substitute "LeBron James" for "our," and Griffin's reasoning makes sense.

Blatt was hired before LeBron decided to take his talents and his ego to Cleveland. Without the King's imprimatur, Blatt was coaching on borrowed time. Even though, in a season and a half, Blatt had compiled an outstanding 83-40 record and brought the Cavs to the 2015 finals without the injured Kevin Love and Kyrie Irving, LBJ's coach of choice was his buddy Tyronn Lue.

Fortunately for LeBron, Lue, and the Cavs, they came back from a 3-1 deficit to dethrone the defending-champion Golden State Warriors in the 2016 Finals. Unfortunately for Blatt, and despite being granted several interviews, he was not offered another NBA coaching job. One interviewer described Blatt as "incredibly nervous." Perhaps not as nervous as Blatt will be in the coaching position he subsequently did take, with Darussafaka Dogus in Turkey.

Hmmm. In a previous discussion about the anti-Semitism Blatt had faced in his various gigs, he said that it was only in the virulently Jew-hating Turkey that he didn't feel safe. Wishing Blatt *iyi sanslar*.

Even so, Blatt has several influential Jews in his corner.

Nachman Shai is the leader of the Zionist Union and the head of the Knesset caucuses on U.S.-Israeli relations and strengthening the Jewish world. After Cleveland won the NBA Championship, he wrote a letter to Dan Gilbert, the Cavs' Jewish owner:

I want to wish you *mazal tov* on your success in bringing a long-awaited championship to the great city of Cleveland and its wonderful people. We in Israel were proud of the achievements of one of our own, David Blatt, when you appointed him as head coach of your team, and we of course were sorry to see him go. Nevertheless, Israelis remain strong supporters of the Cavaliers, as do their many fans in Cleveland's strong Jewish community.

David played a key role in building the Cavaliers, guiding its players, and helping the team become championship-caliber. That is why I want to encourage you to give David the respect and credit he deserves by giving him a championship ring, as is customary for players who have left in mid-season. I am sure he would cherish such a ring that would symbolize his part in your team's success.

The rumor is that the letter has been forwarded to the real *mocher* in the organization for his royal consideration.

24

....

NBA Owners and Bigwigs

As has been said, the parlay of basketball and business has resulted in an overwhelming number of Jews who either owned outright or co-owned NBA teams. Beginning with Max Winter who owned the Minneapolis Lakers in the heyday of George Mikan, an edited list of current (noted by an asterisk) and recent hoop moneymen is still a lengthy one.

Leslie Alexander*—Houston Rockets

Paul Allen—Portland Trail Blazers

Mickey Arison*—Miami Heat

Steve Balmer*—Los Angeles Clippers

Steve Belkin—Atlanta Hawks

Alan Cohen—Boston Celtics, New Jersey Nets, New York Knicks

Mark Cuban*—Dallas Mavericks

William Davidson—Detroit Pistons

Richard Devos—Philadelphia Sixers

Michael Gearon—Atlanta Hawks

Dan Gilbert*—Cleveland Cavaliers

Tom Gores*—Detroit Pistons

Ed Gottlieb owned and coached the Philadelphia Warriors and was infamous for being a world-class cheapskate. On several occasions when he drove from Philadelphia to New York but arrived at Madison Square Garden too early, he'd drive around the block until six when the parking meters no longer required five cents per hour to park. His excuse was that "gas is cheaper."

H. Irving Grousbeck—Boston Celtics

Peter Guber and Joe Lacob*—Golden State Warriors

Lester Harrison was the owner/coach of the Rochester Royals. In 1946 when the Royals were still in the National Basketball League, he made the radical move of signing Dolly King, a black player from LIU, and giving him substantial playing time.

After the Royals joined the NBA, the penny-pinching Harrison refused to provide the traditional orange slices for visiting teams during halftimes. Plus, he personally checked visitors' luggage as they left the arena after games to make sure they weren't stealing any basketballs.

Arnold Heft—Baltimore Bullets. Strangely enough, Heft quickly sold his share of the team and became a highly respected NBA ref for many years.

Michael Heisley—Memphis Grizzlies

George Kaiser*—Oklahoma City Thunder

Ben Kerner—St. Louis Hawks. It was Kerner who traded the draft rights to Bill Russell to Boston (for Ed Macauley), because Russell's NBA debut would be delayed since he was playing in the 1956 Olympic Games in Melbourne, because Russell demanded a salary of twenty thousand dollars, and because Kerner had similar racist beliefs as many residents of St. Louis.

Herb Kohl*—Milwaukee Bucks

Marvin Kratter—Boston Celtics

Stan Kroenke*—Denver Nuggets

Irving Levin—Boston Celtics, Buffalo Braves, Los Angeles Clippers

Abe Polin—Washington Wizards

Mikhail Prokhorov*—Brooklyn Nets

Antony Ressler—Atlanta Hawks

Robert Sarvar*—Phoenix Suns, who for no given reason suddenly fired the wheelchair-bound Neal Walk from his position as the Suns' video man.

Robert Schmertz—Boston Celtics

Howard Schultz—Seattle SuperSonics

Herb Simon*—Indiana Pacers

Ed Snider—Philadelphia Sixers

Donald Sterling—Los Angeles Clippers

Lawrence Tannenbaum—Toronto Raptors

Glen Taylor—Minnesota Timberwolves

Larry Weinberg—Portland Trail Blazers

Let's take a closer look, however, at one of the most successful owners, Jerry Reinsdorf. "I'm just a fat Jewish kid from Brooklyn,"

Reinsdorf likes to say. "I'm only interested in winning championships and I don't care what anybody thinks of me."

Nevertheless, because he's the high-profile managing partner of both the Chicago Bulls and the Chicago White Sox, Reinsdorf is often thought of as being the single most powerful man in professional sports. Because Reinsdorf's personal fortune approaches eighty million dollars and he owns six NBA Championship rings, he is also perceived to be that most heroic of American icons—a winner. And contrary to his avowed disregard of public opinion, Reinsdorf yearns to be seen as an honest businessman trying to maintain personal and financial integrity in a sports world gone mad.

Truth, like beauty, is in the eye of the beholder. The evidence indicates that Reinsdorf's reputation as a winner was, in fact, built on the unexpected genius of Bulls coach Phil Jackson. Similarly, Reinsdorf's reputation as a brilliant power broker is founded on a dubious premise—his convincing the other baseball owners to force the ultimately unsuccessful, and highly unpopular, Major League Baseball strike/lockout of 1994. In reality, Jerry Reinsdorf is just another self-serving financier.

Reinsdorf grew up in Brooklyn, where his father was a sewing-machine repairman. Young Jerry's first business venture was buying firecrackers in Chinatown and then selling them to his eighth grade classmates. Years later, after he graduated from Northwestern Law School, Reinsdorf's first grown-up job was with an outfit that *always* wins—the Internal Revenue Service. The initial source of Reinsdorf's riches was Balcor, Inc., a real estate investment firm he established in 1973. Nine years later he sold Balcor to American Express for $35 million, staying on as CEO until 1987—overseeing $6 billion in real estate deals and earning $50 million in commissions. Yet shortly after he left the firm, disgruntled investors instituted what amounted to $3 billion in lawsuits, charging Balcor with squandering pension funds and with "fraud and racketeering," accusations based on deals made while Reinsdorf was in command. Balcor and its investors lost $300 million, while Reinsdorf skated free. "I was just an employee," he said in his defense.

In January 1981 Reinsdorf put together a partnership that bought the White Sox for $19 million. For his part in formulating the deal, he was allowed to purchase 12 percent of the ball club and was also granted control of baseball operations. But despite the fact that the White Sox won a divisional championship in 1984 (ending a twenty-four-year drought), the Chicago fans became deeply offended, and game attendance suffered dramatically, when Reinsdorf tried to increase his profit margin by moving many of the team's games from free TV to cable. To make matters worse, Reinsdorf drove away legendary play-by-play man Harry Caray to the archrival Cubs.

With his popularity seriously eroded, and the team's financial prospects suddenly looking dim, Reinsdorf feared he'd lose the franchise. To ensure his status as a major-league sports mogul, he assembled another group to buy the struggling Bulls in 1974 (just before MJ ascended into the NBA). As before, Reinsdorf parlayed his organizational skills and only a 10 percent share into unilateral control of the ball club.

Reinsdorf certainly showed a winner's touch in the deals he brokered for new arenas for his two teams. The United Center (which the Bulls share with the NHL's Chicago Blackhawks), for example, cost the same amount of money to build as two other local projects, the Arlington International Racecourse and the Presidential Towers apartment complex. But whereas those two pay $5 million annually in real estate taxes, the United Center's yearly tax obligation is only $1 million. In addition, part of the Bulls' deal includes ticket subsidies from the state. Furthermore, if a lightbulb goes out in a bathroom, the state pays for the bulb and the installation. Counting the gate, concessions, TV money, and the worldwide sale of Bulls paraphernalia, the franchise's annual gross income approaches $225 million.

If the taxpayers of Illinois accepted the terms of Michael Jordan's new playhouse, they resented the crude power play Reinsdorf used to cajole the state legislature into financing a new ballpark for his White

Sox. Illinois's governor, Jim Thompson (a law-school buddy), told Reinsdorf that the only way to be granted the necessary tax money was to threaten to move the White Sox out of town—which Reinsdorf did, claiming he'd relocate the team to St. Petersburg, Florida. Though he later swore his threat was only "make-believe," it proved real enough for Thompson's legislative "arm-twisting" to produce the desired results. (Reinsdorf's cause may have been abetted by his standard practice of making significant political contributions to both parties.) So the taxpayers became responsible for the $500 million cost of what was then known as the new Comiskey Park as well as the $5 million in yearly upkeep. Even though the legislature voted for a severe reduction in state funding for public schools, Reinsdorf got himself another sweetheart deal.

It may be that the proliferation of dollar signs indicates the monumental nature of Jerry Reinsdorf's triumphs. But lurking beneath the diamond glitter is a perpetual tone of discontent.

Years before Reinsdorf took over the Chicago Bulls, Jerry Krause (another Jew) had been the team's general manager under the previous ownership. But Krause had been fired for lying—offering the Bulls' coaching job to DePaul's Ray Meyer and then strongly denying the offer in the face of overwhelming proof to the contrary. Sam Smith, sportswriter for the *Chicago Tribune* and a veteran Bulls watcher, has his own opinion (seconded by many others in the Bulls organization) as to why Reinsdorf chose to resurrect Krause's career: "Reinsdorf makes all of the important decisions concerning the Bulls. Salary. Personnel. Trades. Everything. Krause is basically a bad people-person, and Reinsdorf knows that. But Reinsdorf needs a Secret Service guy to jump in front of him and catch the bullet. Part of Krause's value is that he's such an easy target for the players and for the media. With impeccable loyalty, Krause will do anything to protect his boss."

After suffering through several unsatisfactory seasons under head coaches Kevin Loughery and then Stan Albeck, Reinsdorf empowered his puppet, Krause, to deliberately seek "outlaws," unsavory coaching candidates who would presumably be totally beholden to Krause and Reinsdorf—their saviors. First there was Doug Collins, a one-time NBA All-Star who was an assistant at Arizona State in head coach Bob Weinhauer's notoriously crooked program. Deeply implicated in several shady recruiting practices, Collins got out of town one step ahead of the NCAA's investigators.

But Collins wasn't as easily controlled as Krause and Reinsdorf had anticipated. It turned out that Collins constantly battled with his assistants, vocally dissed many of his players, ignored defense, substituted a play of the week for any comprehensive game plan, and was a prima donna whose primary assets were a winning smile and the ability to manipulate the media. Collins came to be perceived as a loose cannon by Reinsdorf and Krause (known to the local media as "the two Jerrys") and was fired immediately after the 1988–89 season.

Collins's replacement, Phil Jackson, had been a Bulls assistant for two years, but was hired as head coach because he, too, was on the outside of the basketball establishment. A onetime hippie whose autobiography, *Maverick*, disclosed several acid trips, Jackson was generally considered to be too much the iconoclast to be entrusted with an NBA team. Ironically, however, Jackson was the right coach even though he was originally hired for the wrong reasons. And as Jackson won more and more NBA Championships, he became less and less obligated to his superiors. Meanwhile, both Reinsdorf and Krause wanted to be publicly celebrated as the prime movers behind the Bulls' spectacular successes and became increasingly jealous of Jackson's popularity with the players, the fans, and especially the media. Indeed, Jackson's contract was not renewed after the 1997–98 season, only to be replaced by Tim Floyd out of Iowa State. Unfortunately for the two Jerrys, Floyd was a total flop in the NBA.

Reinsdorf's obsession with receiving kudos for the Bulls' achievements even managed to alienate the seemingly unflappable Michael Jordan. Several Bulls insiders reported that one significant reason Jordan opted to leave the team and play baseball in 1993 was that both Reinsdorf and Krause privately boasted that the Bulls didn't need their superstar and could continue winning championships with the self-indulgent Toni Kuko as their go-to player. This never happened. But those who know Reinsdorf best say that he's a kindly man who enjoys simple pleasures like smoking cigars and watching baseball games on TV. He's also comfortable buying his own groceries and steering a shopping cart through a supermarket. And he looks forward to driving by himself to and from his permanent home in Phoenix.

Fiscally conservative, Reinsdorf believes that free agency is destroying professional sports. Modern players are mercenaries who have no loyalties to any organization and are motivated only by greed. That's why the fans can't keep track of who's playing where and don't understand why mediocre athletes are signed to multimillion-dollar contracts. Reinsdorf sees himself as a light in the darkness, an honorable man who stubbornly, and righteously, insists on making rational business decisions in an irrational, emotional sports culture. "Reinsdorf is a gentle man," says Phil Jackson, "and he feels there's a moral basis for generating money. He also believes that profit is the ultimate barometer for measuring success in any field."

Even so, Reinsdorf has few friends among the ruling circles of both the NBA and the major leagues. The Lords of Baseball were appalled at his failure to cover his tracks when arbitrator George Nicolau investigated charges that baseball conspired not to sign free agents in 1985 and 1986. Most damaging was a careless phone call Reinsdorf made to owner Bill Giles, dissuading the Phillies from signing Lance Parish in the name of fiscal responsibility. The phone call was a major factor that ultimately led to a judgment costing the owners $280 million in fines. A veteran owner of a National League team called out Reinsdorf's hypocrisy: "First he sold all of us on the necessity of cutting down players' salaries, then he signed Albert Belle for five years and fifty-five million. Man, did Reinsdorf piss us off!"

In the summer of 1997 Reinsdorf made a patently cheap and immoral decision that made patsies of Chicago's sports fans. Interleague play had just been initiated, and Reinsdorf refused to sell individual tickets to the Sox-Cubs games that were played at the new Comiskey Park. In order to witness these historic contests, those who were not season ticket holders were compelled to buy a package of tickets to three other games. Reinsdorf defended his attempted extortion by claiming that the idea was to keep Cubs fans from attending the games and rooting against the White Sox. The baseball fans revolted, and ticket sales were so slow that Reinsdorf was forced to surrender.

Nor were his NBA colleagues fond of Reinsdorf's financial machinations. This was especially so after he filed a lawsuit against the NBA in 1990 when the league tried to limit the number of Bulls games nationally broadcast over superstation WGN. The league's reasoning was that these games would curtail interest and attendance in other NBA cities.

The suit, which was finally settled in December 1996, cost the league an estimated $10 million in legal fees. Even worse, evidence revealed during the case led to the discovery by the NBA Players' Association that some owners were underreporting revenues in an attempt to lower the salary cap. Facing another round of litigation, NBA officials hurriedly worked out a $60 million settlement with the players.

"Suing the NBA," said Jerry Colangelo, at the time the owner of the Phoenix Suns, "was no way to deal with his partners. There's only one way to describe Jerry Reinsdorf's actions—*greed*."

In his private life Reinsdorf may indeed be a compassionate and generous man. But once there's money on the line, Jerry Reinsdorf firmly believes that what's good for the Bulls and the White Sox is good for America. Nevertheless, he was voted into basketball's Naismith Hall of Fame in 2016.

Testimony: Race Rules

An unsigned article, "The Complete Infestation of the NBA by Jews," was posted on the *Race Rules* blog on Christmas Day 2011. Here are two excerpts that should serve to remind one and all that hatred still has a loud voice:

After listing the known NBA owners, the writer says that he "could not find any info on four [other] owners . . . but cowardly crypto-Jews are everywhere. . . . Many times they change their names or even occasionally breed with Gentiles to throw us off the scent." In conclusion:

Why do Jews only want to dominate sports, media, porn and the Federal Reserve? Because money is their religion and the media controls the mind. It's that simple. They distract and corrupt. They actually own all the religions as well. Americans are such dumb asses. We could end all of this tomorrow but we believe that we have to continue spiraling down this chasm in the hopes of saving our individual asses while everyone else perishes. Divide and conquer always works on Americans who have absolutely no sense of unity on anything except buying more useless shit. We think we can beat the system if we work hard enough and kiss enough asses. Well you can't. It's all rigged by the Jewish elite and their asskissers so you may as well stop trying and wasting your time. If you are not one of them you don't get it. Get it through your thick skull. They don't care if you won a hundred million in the lottery. Jews promote Jews and Jews only, and not even those that convert like dumb-ass Amare Stoudamire [*sic*], only the European Ashkenazim from the proper inbred bloodline. That's why they're so damn butt-ass ugly too. With all that money you would think they would get some plastic surgery but that's probably some depopulation technique reserved solely for Gentiles. In conclusion FUCK THE NBA!!!!!! Every American should just turn it off. These owners are the subhumans destroying the world and the players are okay with it as long as they get paid just like Hollywood stars and just like the federal government and most likely just like you for your paycheck. We did it to ourselves by taking orders from them and bowing to their Satanic money god.

25

....

Recent Notable Players

After the "Molinas scandals," there were several more Jews who played a minimum of twenty-five games in either the NBA or the ABA or the leagues combined. Players already mentioned—Larry Brown, Rudy LaRusso, Neal Walk, et al.—are not listed herein.

Note: ABA teams are marked with an asterisk.

Howard Carl—DePaul; Chicago Packers (1961–62)

Steve Chubin—Rhode Island; Anaheim Amigos*, Los Angeles Stars*, Minnesota Pipers*, Indiana Pacers*, New Jersey Nets*, Pittsburgh Pipers*, Kentucky Colonels* (1967–70). That's eight teams in three seasons, which must be some kind of record. Through it all Chubin's career point-per-game average was a more than respectable 12.8.

Barry Clemens—Ohio Wesleyan; New York Knicks, Chicago Bulls, Seattle SuperSonics, Cleveland Cavaliers, Portland Trail Blazers (1965–76)

Jerry Greenspan—Maryland; Philadelphia Warriors (1963–65)

Ernie Grunfeld—Tennessee; Milwaukee Bucks, Kansas City Kings, New York Knicks (1977–86). Born in Romania,

Grunfeld and Bernard King were the celebrated "Ernie and Bernie Show" at Tennessee. As of this writing, Grunfeld is the long-term general manager of the Washington Wizards.

Art Heyman—Duke; New York Knicks, Cincinnati Royals, New Jersey Americans*, Pittsburgh/Minnesota Pipers*, Miami Floridians* (1963–66, 1967–70). At Duke Heyman was a three-time All-American and was selected by several media outlets as the College Player of the Year in 1963.

Barry Kramer—NYU; San Francisco Warriors, New York Knicks, New York Nets* (1964–65, 1969–70)

Joel Kramer—San Diego State; Phoenix Suns (1978–83)

Barry Liebowitz—LIU; Oakland Oaks*, New Jersey Americans*, Pittsburgh Pipers* (1967–68)

Gal Mekel was born in Israel and subsequently played at Wichita State and then with the Dallas Mavericks and the New Orleans Pelicans. Unfortunately, the six-foot-three point guard was a bust in the NBA (2013–15), averaging 9.6 minutes, 2.3 points, and 2.2 assists in thirty-five games. While Mekel did prove to be an excellent passer, he was also revealed to be a terrible shooter—21.7 percent from downtown and 31.1 percent overall.

Dave Newmark—Columbia; Chicago Bulls, Atlanta Hawks, Carolina Cougars (1968–71). A notorious free spirit, Newmark signed a contract for two hundred thousand dollars when the Bulls drafted him in the third round (thirty-first overall) in 1968. Newmark then proudly announced that he spent half of his money on marijuana.

Danny Schayes—Syracuse; Utah Jazz, Denver Nuggets, Milwaukee Bucks, Los Angeles Lakers, Phoenix Suns, Miami Heat, Orlando Magic (1981–99). Son of Dolph, Danny also coached the gold-medal-winning U.S. basketball team in the 1977 Maccabiah Games.

Ron Watts—Wake Forest; Boston Celtics (1965–67)

Rick Weitzman—Northeastern; Boston Celtics (1987–88). For many years after his brief playing career ended, Weitzman scouted for several NBA teams.

Dave Wohl—Pennsylvania; Philadelphia Sixers, Portland Trail Blazers, Buffalo Braves, Houston Rockets, New York Knicks, New Jersey Nets (1971–78).

In addition, besides those listed above, there have been a handful of other Jewish All-Americans in the last forty years of the twentieth century.

Sue Bird won several honors at the University of Connecticut, including the Wade Trophy and the Naismith Award for being the best women's college player in 2002. Shortly thereafter, she was the first pick in the WNBA's draft and then has been a seven-time league All-Star with the Seattle Storm. In her off-seasons from 2004 to 2007, Bird has played in Russia.

Tal Brody graduated from the University of Illinois in 1965, and the Baltimore Bullets made him the twelfth all-around pick in the subsequent NBA draft. However, after leading the U.S. squad to a gold medal in the 1965 Maccabiah Games, Brody chose to stay in Israel. He soon became one of the country's most outstanding players and was Israel's high scorer in the 1969 Maccabiah Games when they upset the U.S. team to cop the gold.

Rick Kaminsky at Yale (1961–64). He was selected in the sixth round by Philadelphia (forty-ninth overall) but never played in the NBA.

Steve Nisenson scored 2,222 career points at Hofstra in three varsity seasons without the benefit of the three-point line (1962–65).

Donna Orender was an All-American at Queens College (1978). Using the name Donna Giles, she then went on to play in the WNBA for the New York Stars, New Jersey Gems, and Chicago Hustle (1978–81), where she was a three-time All-Star. After becoming a professional golfer, she returned to the WNBA as president of the league (2005–10). These days Orender is involved in producing TV shows as well as media marketing.

Testimony: The Referees

If Nate Messinger and Sol Levy gave Jewish referees a bad name, several of their landsmen who worked the same beat resurrected this unfortunate reputation.

Norm Drucker played under Nat Holman at CCNY (1940–42) before enlisting in the army. He continued his playing career in the New York State Professional League and then in the ABL. After his playing days were done, and still wanting to be a part of the sport he loved, in 1949 Drucker began officiating AAU, high school, and ABL games. His reputation was so sterling that he was asked to substitute for an ailing NBA ref for a single game in 1951. Two years later Drucker became a full-fledged NBA official.

In 1969 Drucker and three other "lead" officials jumped to the ABA, only to return to the NBA six years later when the two leagues merged.

During one NBA game in the early 1960s, Drucker had some trouble with his equipment. *New York Daily News* sportswriter Vic Ziegel wrote the following limerick to explain the situation:

Norm Drucker lost his whistle
Couldn't tweet and couldn't twistle

Used his voice as a substitute
For all the missing root-toot-toot
(Of course it hurt his throat a bissel)

Drucker's son, Jim, was the commissioner of the Continental Basketball Association from 1978 to 1986.

Other Jewish game officials include Lou Eisenstein; Phil Fox, who also worked several Maccabiah Games; the aforementioned Arnold Heft; Sam Schoenfeld; Jack Silverman; Manny Sokol; and Stan Stutz, the first former player to become a referee.

Marat Kogut's family emigrated from the Ukraine in 1979 to escape the latest outbreak of virulent anti-Semitism there. Marat was two months old when they arrived in New York, and until his father found work as a barber, the family lived in a Queens homeless shelter. Shortly thereafter, his father had saved up enough money to buy his own shop.

After graduating from St. John's, Kogut enrolled in several referee schools, where his diligence, knowledge of the rules, and decision making impressed his instructors. By 2004 he was working D League as well as WNBA games. Five years later Kogut graduated into the NBA and has remained there ever since, comfortably situated with an annual salary of ninety thousand dollars, plus a per diem of three hundred dollars for food and hotels.

The best Jewish referee (and arguably the best NBA ref ever) has to be Marvin "Mendy" Rudolph. From 1953 to 1977 Rudolph was a mainstay of the NBA's refereeing corps. During that time he was selected to work in eight All-Star Games and made 22 consecutive appearances in championship series. Overall, he officiated 2,112 NBA games.

I caught up with Rudolph in his office at 1 Penn Plaza just as the 1973–74 season was under way. Mounted on the wall of the surprisingly modestly furnished office were several photographs, most of them showing Rudolph in various game situations: going face-to-chest with Wilt Chamberlain; doing his patented hands-on-hips shuffle to indicate a blocking foul; a shot from behind him as he studies the game action, with his famous uniform number 5 patched near the top of his striped shirt.

For the interview he wore tasseled black loafers, gray slacks, and a blue Ban-Lon shirt that emphasized his trim physique. Despite his rather pedestrian clothing, Rudolph managed to look classy and resplendent.

Since I was in my slightly belligerent hippie phase, I was wearing sneakers, faded blue jeans, a tie-dyed T-shirt, and love beads. Of course, my hair was long, and my beard was bushy. Before we even shook hands, this is what Rudolph said to me: "Who's your tailor?"

"Ha ha," I said.

He glanced at his gold-banded wristwatch, and then we settled down into a traditional Q&A interview.

Q: "Why did you become a referee?"

A: "I was born in Philadelphia in 1926 and lived there throughout most of my life. My father, Harry, was a highly respected basketball referee and baseball umpire in the area. I wasn't much of a ballplayer, but my father taught me the love of sports, especially basketball. So it was a natural thing for me to continue the family tradition. I started officiating basketball games in the Wilkes-Barre Jewish Community Center, and then moved on to high school games."

Q: "From there?"

A: "Well, Eddie Gottlieb had seen me work in the Philadelphia area and recommended me to Maurice Podoloff. Before long, I was fortunate enough to move up to the NBA."

Q: "What do you see as your basic job during a game?"

A: "To choreograph an athletic event. To give the world's greatest athletes an even playing field where they can show their skills."

Q: "It seems to me that refs must necessarily focus on mistakes and misplays, so they miss much of the beauty of the game."

A: "A beautiful game is when it's over, and nobody—not the players, not the coaches, not the fans, not the media—can remember who the officials were. A beautiful game is when we disappear as individuals and only the justice of the calls we make survives."

Q: "But no matter how just those calls might be, there will be players, coaches, fans, and media who will strongly disagree."

A: "That's because they have a bias. They care who wins and who loses, but we couldn't care less about what the scoreboard says."

Q: "But it's well known that certain refs are homers, that some always favor the better teams, that superstars can get away with things, and that some will go out of their way to avoid a blowout."

A: "Nonsense. We travel so much that most of the time, we don't even know what city we're in."

Q: "But the home teams always wear white uniforms."

A: "We don't have time to check out the color of the uniforms when we blow a whistle. Anyway, better teams are more efficient and make fewer mistakes than bad teams. And players are called superstars because they're also more efficient and mistake free than other players. As far as deliberately making calls to avoid blowouts . . . First of all, we never look at the scoreboard. And second, the shot clock gives teams ample opportunity to catch up."

Q: "What about makeup calls?"

A: "There's no such thing, because that would be making two bad calls in a row. That's like if a student fails a math test, then in his next class deliberately fails a history test. It makes no sense. But you have to realize that NBA officials make the right call over 90 percent of the time."

Q: "What about the no-calls that should be made?"

A: "We can't call what we can't see. Especially as the player get bigger and the court gets more crowded. That's why I've been lobbying so hard for three officials."

Q: "What about . . . ?"

A: "Listen, Charley. I've got a meeting in a few minutes. You've got all you need, right?"

Q: "I guess so. Anything you want to say to sum things up"

A: "Sure . . . I'd just say that NBA officials have the judgment of Supreme Court justices."

Rudolph passed away in July 1979, and David Stern promised to retire his number 5. However, in 2009 Kane Fitzgerald was given the once-celebrated number 5, which he still wears. How quickly, in the fast-paced, madcap, not-always-so-wonderful world of the NBA, excellence is forgotten!

26

The Jewish Jordan

Back when he was averaging 35.4 points per game in his junior year at the Talmudical Academy of Baltimore, Tamir Goodman favored a blue yarmulke that made his red hair seem almost incandescent. And he had all the moves—tricky behind-the-back dribbles, crossovers where he seemed to have the ball on a string, stop-and-goes as quick and explosive as the Road Runner, spinning the rock on one finger and then flipping it to another finger on his other hand, plus a variety of dunks ranging from fancy to savage. Eagle-eyed scouts rated him the twenty-fifth best high school player in the country.

One of Tamir's buddies made a video of Goodman dancing his way through the young man's hip-hop one-on-none basketball drills, accompanied by a bouncy rap lyric entitled "The Yid with a Lid."

Even though the inter-Judaic high school competition was awful, Goodman's numbers and his shtick were impressive. They were impressive enough for *Sports Illustrated*, in its February 1999 issue, to dub Goodman "the Jewish Jordan" and impressive enough for ESPN and *60 Minutes* to also feature him.

However, the rabbis who ran the Talmudic Academy were not at all impressed. Moreover, they were so horrified at all the publicity that they terminated the school's basketball program. Nor was Goodman's mother very enthusiastic about all the hoops hoopla.

"Basketball," she shrugged. "It's nonsense, but if that's what Tamir wants . . ."

Yet Gary Williams, coach of the powerhouse Maryland Terrapins, was so impressed that he offered Goodman a full scholarship, which the youngster eagerly accepted on one important condition: as an Orthodox Jew, Goodman would not be permitted to play from sundown on Fridays to sundown on Saturdays. Williams hemmed, hawed, and vaguely suggested that something could be worked out.

But Maryland's schedule was never altered, and it appeared that the scholarship offer was nothing more than a publicity stunt. Instead of Maryland, Goodman accepted a full ride from nearby Towson State, where he became the first freshman to start for the varsity in the previous eleven years. Playing under coach Mike Jaskulski, Goodman's per-game numbers for that season were 6 points, 4 assists, and 2.5 rebounds. They were good enough for Goodman to receive the Coach's Award for his performance on the court and in the classroom. Even so, after the team finished at 12-17, the only postseason award that Jaskulski received was a pink slip.

While he and Jaskulski had a good relationship, Goodman and his new coach, Michael Hunt, didn't connect. According to Goodman, for some reason he never revealed, Hunt got so angry at something Tamir had done that he held a chair over the young man's head and kicked a stool that crashed into his leg. At that point Goodman quit the team and left the school. "After that happened," Goodman said several years later, "I was completely broken, spiritually and physically. I wanted nothing to do with basketball anymore. I was down. I was really, really down."

It didn't take long, though, for Goodman to regain his passion for the sport. He started training, going through his flashy drills, until he regained his chops. But where could he play? If he enrolled in another school, under the NCAA rules he would be forced to sit out a year before becoming eligible. So he decided to turn pro. Goodman knew that playing in the NBA was a pipe dream, so he connected with an Israeli ball club—Maccabi Tel Aviv.

This seemed to be an incredible opportunity. Imagine—getting paid to play while living in the Holy Land! So, on July 22, 2002, the twenty-year-old Goodman signed a three-year contract and moved to Israel.

Too bad his game wasn't up to it. The story was that Goodman, in order to get more playing time, was "loaned" to Giv'at Shmuel for the 2002–3 season and then to Elitzur Kiryat Atat the following season.

As an Israeli citizen Goodman went on to serve in the military, but upon his release he suffered a knee injury that required major surgery. With his recovery still incomplete, Goodman signed with Maccabi Shoham, a team in a lower classification. His knee held up for two games in which he totaled nearly forty points. But in December 2006 his knee gave out again.

This round of rehab was longer and more painful than before. Disenchanted with his professional career in Israel, Goodman returned to Baltimore in December 2007. He vowed to give himself one more chance and signed with the Maryland Nighthawks in the newly formed and short-lived Premier Basketball League. In his very first game Goodman suffered a serious hand injury that required another round of surgery and rehabilitation.

Still undaunted, he returned to Israel in July 2008 to play for Maccabi Haifa, but shattered several bones in his left hand during a practice session.

And that was that. Since then Goodman has remained in Israel and undertaken simultaneous careers in motivational speaking in places as far away from Israel and Baltimore as China. In partnership with Omri Casspi, Goodman has also founded several nonprofit basketball camps designed to bring Jewish and Arab kids together. He is also the author of *The Jewish Jordan's Triple Threat* as well as the inventor of Zone190, a training device.

These days Goodman lives with his wife and four children in Jerusalem and looks back on his days as a celebrity with a mixture of remorse, confusion, and acceptance. "When I go to check my bags at an airport," he says, "I've had baggage handlers identify me as the

Jewish Jordan. That whole business really impacted my entire life. I never asked to put it on myself, and when I was young I really didn't know how to deal with it, or how to deal with my injuries."

Eventually, Goodman came to terms with his own life. "All my injuries were the biggest blessings," he says, "because in the early part of my career, I had tremendous amounts of success. And how can you inspire someone if you've never had to struggle yourself? Society tends to, for basketball players, define success as 'How many points do you score?' For me, I've learned that success is what good you can do for someone through basketball."

Tamir Goodman is another victim of the sports media that is perpetually seeking another Michael Jordan or Babe Ruth. "Hopefully," he says, "one day I'll get a chance to meet Michael Jordan."

And what would he do if this connection ever does happen? His answer demonstrates Tamir Goodman's humility and the awareness of his many blessings: "I would apologize."

Testimony: Barry Kramer

Barry Kramer played big-time basketball at NYU while I was playing small-time basketball at Hunter College. So even though we were both lived and played in New York City, it's understandable why I saw him play dozens of times on TV and he never witnessed any of my games.

But we did get to play on the same team. Once, that is, when we were both in our early fifties and I was a member of the Albany Golden Bears.

The occasion was a scrimmage between the Bears and a pickup team of younger players. The idea was to have a get-to-know-you session between Barry and the Bears in preparation for our participating in the over-fifty classification of the World Senior Games to be held in St. George, Utah. It turned out that Barry couldn't join us, but we eventually won a bronze medal anyway.

However, from the first play my new (and temporary) teammate and I were in perfect synch. We both zigged and zagged with uncanny coordination. Every backdoor cut was rewarded with a perfect pass and an easy hoop. Screens were set at the perfect times and in perfect places. Rolls, slipped screens, faked curls and dive cuts, lob passes, lead passes—all on the money. It was as though we'd been playing together for decades. It was an extremely enjoyable and memorable experience for both of us.

Some twenty-two years later Barry and I reconnected in a phone conversation that was speckled with fond reminiscences. I remember having been impressed with his shooting and his ops. He recalled my passing, rebounding, and strength.

That was then. Now I was seventy-five, a former CBA coach, and a fairly successful freelance writer. Barry was Judge Kramer, a New York Supreme Court justice in the Eleventh Judicial District. "My jurisprudence extends from Schenectady to the Canadian border," he says. "And my normal caseload is anywhere from 750 to 1,000. And I love this job."

Even so, we were more anxious to talk about basketball. Since Mendy Rudolph had told me that NBA referees had the judgment of Supreme Court justices, it seemed appropriate to ask Kramer a pertinent question. "For sure, in Adam Silver, the NBA has another Jewish commissioner, but in this past 2015–16 season, Omri Casspi and Jordan Farmar were the only Jewish players. Why don't Jews play basketball anymore?"

"When we were both kids, Charley, there was always a playground or a schoolyard basketball court within a short walk. So we played ball whenever we could. Five, six hours a day. No uniforms, no coaches, no refs. Just basketball. And if the games weren't so good at one place, we walk over and play somewhere else. Right?"

"Absolutely."

"But these kids nowadays have computers and iPods, and they need to be transported to play any kind of sport. Only in the inner cities are there basketball courts as readily available as they used to be for us."

Even after he donned his judicial robes, Kramer would go from one court to another after work. "I played into my sixties," he says, "until things got out of hand. Guys would bring guns to the games, and there would be fights. I didn't want to quit, but I had to wean myself away from playing."

Yet he still misses the action. "I have dreams where I'm getting another chance to play in the NBA. I've come to training camp and I'm lacing up my sneakers when I suddenly realize that I'm too old to do this. It's a big disappointment."

In fact, Kramer's abbreviated NBA career was a disappointment that still rankles him. "I badly sprained my ankle in my senior season at NYU, and it took about a year to fully heal. Then I got drafted by the San Francisco Warriors, whose coach, Alex Hannum, was an anti-Semite. He'd complain about the general manager sending him a Jew, and he just never gave me a chance."

Kramer averaged 3.1 points and 8.4 minutes in thirty-three games for the Warriors. "But I know I could play at that level. I mean, I had a nose for scoring. Anyway, midway through the season I was traded to the Knicks, but I was so discouraged that I didn't play well in New York. After that I played some games in the Eastern League and in the ABA. Since then it's been in the parks and playgrounds of Albany."

And Barry Kramer also wonders what would have been different if his first NBA coach hadn't hated Jews. "Fifty years later," he says, "I still have a sick feeling about it. I guess Jews and basketball are not as good a mix as they used to be."

This court is adjourned.

APPENDIX

Jews in the Naismith Hall of Fame

PLAYERS

Sam Balter
Davey Banks (enshrined as
    a member of the Original
    Celtics)
Max "Marty" Friedman
Nat Holman
Nancy Lieberman
Dolph Schayes
Barney Sedran
Ed Wachter

COACHES

Arnold "Red" Auerbach
Larry Brown
William "Red" Holzman
Harry Litwack
Leonard Sachs

REFEREES

Bennie Borgman
Mendy Rudolph
David "Pep" Tobey

CONTRIBUTORS

Senda Berenson
Harry F. Fisher
Larry Fleisher
Leo Gottlieb
Russ Granick
Lester Harrison
Maurice Podoloff
Jerry Reindorf
Abe Saperstein
Edward Steitz
David Stern

SOURCES

Broussard, Chris. "Pro Basketball: Comments by 2 Knicks Called Anti-Semitic."
    New York Times, April 21, 2001. http://www.nytimes.com/2001/04/21
    /sports/pro-basketball-comments-by-2-knicks-called-anti-semitic.html.
Butnick, Stephanie. "Aaron Liberman Makes NCAA Big Ten History." *Tablet*,
    January 7, 2014. http://www.tabletmag.com/scroll/158602/aaron
    -liberman-makes-ncaa-big-ten-history.
———. "Stoudemire Applying for Israeli Citizenship." *Tablet*, August 2, 2013.
    http://www.tabletmag.com/scroll/140093/stoudemire-applying-for
    -israeli-citizenship.
"Cavaliers to Give Blatt Ring." *Jerusalem Post*, June 22, 2016.
"The Complete Infestation of the NBA by Jews." *Race Rules* (blog), December
    25, 2011. https://racerules.wordpress.com/2011/12/25/the-complete
    -infestation-of-jewish-nba-owners/.
Goldstein, Richard. "Red Klotz, Beloved Foil for the Harlem Globetrotters, Dies
    at 93." *New York Times*, July 14, 2014. http://www.nytimes.com/2014/07
    /15/sports/basketball/red-klotz-beloved-foil-for-globetrotters-dies-at-93
    .html.
Grundman, Dolph. *Dolph Schayes and the Rise of Professional Basketball*. Syracuse
    NY: Syracuse University Press, 2014.
Hollander, Zander, ed. *The Modern Encyclopedia of Basketball*. New York:
    Doubleday, 1979.
Isaacs, Neil D. *Vintage NBA*. Indianapolis: Masters Press, 1996.
Jewsinsports.org.
Jewishsports.net/the_maccabiah_games.htm.

Levine, Peter. *Ellis Island to Ebbets Field: Sport and the American Jewish Experience.* New York: Oxford University Press, 1992.

Meany, Jim. "Remembering Lou Sugarman: Syracuse Basketball's First One-and-Done Superstar." Fan post at *Troy Nunes Is an Absolute Magician* (blog), June 19, 2011. http://www.nunesmagician.com/2011/6/19/2230886/remembering-lou-sugarman-syracuse-basketballs-first-one-and-done.

Meiser, Rebecca. "The Jewish Jordan Subs Out." *Tablet*, October 18, 2012. http://www.tabletmag.com/jewish-news-and-politics/114191/the-jewish-jordan-subs-out.

Nathan, Giri. "When NBA Players Go to Israel." *New Yorker*, September 24, 2015. http://www.newyorker.com/news/sporting-scene/when-n-b-a-players-go-to-israel.

Nelson, Murry R. *The National Basketball League: A History, 1935–1949.* Jefferson NC: McFarland, 2009.

Postal, Bernard, Jesse Silver, and Roy Silver. *Encyclopedia of Jews in Sports.* New York: Bloch, 1965.

Rosen, Charley. *The First Tip-Off: The Incredible Story of the Birth of the NBA.* New York: McGraw-Hill, 2009.

———. *The Scandals of '51: How the Gamblers Almost Killed College Basketball.* New York: Seven Stories Press, 1978.

Shouler, Ken, Bob Ryan, Sam Smith, Leonard Koppett, and Bob Bellotti. *Total Basketball: The Ultimate Basketball Encyclopedia.* Toronto: Sport Classic Books, 2003.

Siegman, Joseph. *Jewish Sporting Legends: The International Jewish Sports Hall of Fame.* 2nd ed. Washington DC: Brassey's, 1997.

Stark, Douglas. *Wartime Basketball.* Lincoln: University of Nebraska Press, 2016.

Stoke, Pat M. "The NBA Finals: Anti-Semitic Conspiracy?" *The Mideast Beast*, April 19, 2016. http://www.themideastbeast.com/nba-finals-anti-semitic-conspiracy/.

Westcott, Rich. *The Mogul: Eddie Gottlieb, Philadelphia Sports Legend and Pro Basketball Pioneer.* Philadelphia: Temple University Press, 2008.

INTERVIEWS

The author conducted interviews with the following people: David Blatt, Hubie Brown, Omri Casspi, Jordan Farmar, Richie Goldberg, Tamir Goodman, Sonny Hill, Barry Kramer, Nancy Lieberman, Ed Roman, Lennie Rosenbluth, Dolph Schayes, Ossie Schectman, Arieh Sclar, David Stern, Amare Stoudemire, and Neal Walk. Many thanks to one and all for their gracious expenditures of time and effort.